DELICIOUS

INSTANT POT RECIPES

Table of Contents

PALEO MASHED DINGHIES

Ingredients
- 2 tablespoons olive oil, shared into two
- 8 diced cloves of garlic
- 2 squash spaghettis, divided and the seed removed

Preparation
- Cut squash into two and take out the seeds with a spoon.
- Put the garlic and olive oil in squash, put on the cookie sheet.
- Bake for one hour at 350, until it gets soft.
- When it is soft, make use of a fork to rake the squash, this will form a spaghetti texture. Take of the up the squash flesh up off the shell.
- Include pesto in the squash and mix together.
- I like adding little grated parmesan and red pepper flakes.

TWO POTS BURRITO DISHES

Ingredients:
- 1 cups of red bell pepper
- 2 cups of jack cheese / shredded cheddar
- 1 teaspoon of chili powder
- 2 pounds thin hamburger
- 1 cup of sweet onion, diced
- 1/4 cup Old El Paso Medium Thick n' Chunky Salsa
- 2 15 oz canned black beans, drained after rinsing
- 2 Tablespoons of olive oil
- 2 14.5 oz of canned chopped tomatoes
- 2 15 oz of canned corn, not wet
- 2 4 oz of canned chopped green chiles by Old El Paso
- 2 cups of jasmine rice (or any long grain)
- 2 Tablespoons of taco seasoning
- 4 cups of chicken stock (you can make use of chicken broth aswell)
- S & P to make it tasty

Optional toppings:
- Green Onions
- Avocado
- Cilantro
- Sour cream
- Tomatoes

Directions:
- Heat the olive oil with medium heat in a big pan. Saute the red peppers and onions. Put in the hamburger and cook till it becomes browned. Stir in black beans, salsa, corn, green chiles, tomatoes, taco seasoning chili powder, and jasmine rice. Pour in the chicken stock and then boil lightly. Close the pan and take the heat reduction to low. Cook for 15-20 minutes extra, or till the rice is well cooked.
- After the rice is done, S&P to make it tasty. Add your best toppings. We like it served in a salad bowl with lettuce and eaten with tortilla chips.

RECIPE FOR RED LENTIL ROOT VEGETABLE SAUCE

Ingredients
- 4 carrots, sliced into pieces 1-inch size.
- 2 sweet potatoes, sliced into pieces 1-inch size.
- 2 tablespoons of coconut oil, ghee, or olive oil.
- 8 Yukon gold potatoes or small red potatoes, sliced into pieces 1-inch size.
- Fresh cilantro
- 4 parsnips, sliced into pieces 1-inch size after peeling.
- 1 big onion well sliced.
- 6 cloves of garlic, crushed.
- 1 1-inch piece of fresh ginger, chopped after peeling.
- 1/2 teaspoon ground coriander.
- Half bunch of kale, finely sliced.
- 3 teaspoons of curry powder.
- 1/4 teaspoon of turmeric.
- 1/2 teaspoon of ground cardamom.
- 1 1/2 teaspoons of sea salt.
- 6 cups of water.
- 1 cup of red lentils.
- Juice of half a lime or lemon.

Preparation

- Get the above listed root vegetables (chop carrots, parsnips, red potatoes and sweet potato after peeling them). Keep them separate in a big bowl.
- Slice the garlic, ginger and onion. In a big pot with medium heat, pour in the onions and oil and a bigger pinch of salt. Mix for 5 minutes till the onions become translucent. Pour in the chopped garlic, ginger and with other spices and stir for 30 seconds till aroma starts coming out.
- Pour in 1 1/2 teaspoons of salt, six cups of water and all the root vegetables with lentils in the pot. Increase the heat till the soup starts boiling. Turn down the heat to low and partially simmer it close it for 30 minutes, turning occasionally. If the stew gets very thick pour more water in it.
- When the root vegetables become tender and lentils are broken down turn the heat off. Pour in the sliced kale inside the pot and turn until it wilts. Pour in the juice of half a lime or lemon and mix. Taste to know if the salt is adequate. Pour into bowls; you can serve it with fresh cilantro on it.

SWEET POTATO WITH PALEO CHICKEN ROAST

You'll need:
- sea salt
- 1 big sweet potatoe, sliced in chunks after washing (I didn't peel off the skin)
- 1/2 pint of tomatoes and grape mixed
- 1 chicken breasts preferably the free range organic
- olive oil
- 2 minced big cloves of garlic, the quantity should be based on your choice
- 1/4 tsp red sliced pepper
- 1 Tbs of Italian seasoning

Method
- In a big ziplock bag, a, pour in small quantity of olive oil, few some spices, and potatoes slice – 2 cloves of garlic which should be minced, 1 tablespoon of salt,1/4 tablespoon of cracked pepper, I tablespoon of Italian spice. Shake ingredients till it is coated. Pour into a baking sheet; bake for about 10 to15 minutes or till the edges start getting brown.
- Pour in 1 tablespoon of Italian spice, ¼ tablespoon of grounded pepper, chicken breasts, half of your spices, and little quantity of oil into the same big ziplock bag. Close and shake the ingredients till it becomes totally coated.
- Pour in little olive oil, and make the chicken brown a bit, in a big skillet with average heat. Your sweet potatoes ought to be done once both sides of the chicken become brown. Take them out of the oven and place them together with the tomatoes in the pans outer edges. Uncover it and cook till the chicken is done or for about 7 to 10 minutes. Shake the pan frequently so that it won't stick. It will be enough to serve two or as you desire.
- This a great dish. It has this autumn feeling that makes you have the cozy and warmth feeling within.

TWO PANS OF ROOT VEGGIES, SAGE, APPLES WITH COOKED PORK TENDERLOIN

Ingredients
- 1-1.5lb pork tenderloin

Roasted vegetables
- 4 sliced cloves garlic,
- 1 medium onion, roughly sliced
- 1 peeled medium apple, roughly sliced
- 8 quartered baby potatoes
- 1/4 tablespoon of salt
- 8 chopped fresh sage leaves, {at least 1 tablespoon}
- 2 tablespoon of apple cider vinegar
- 1 tablespoon white wine
- 2 tablespoon of olive oil
- 6 peeled carrots, roughly sliced
- 3 peeled parsnips, roughly sliced
- 1/4 tablespoon pepper

Glaze/sauce
- 2 tablespoons of Dijon mustard
- 4 tablespoons of applesauce
- 2 tablespoons of apple cider vinegar
- 2 tablespoons of brown sugar

Rub
- 2 tablespoons of brown sugar
- 1 tablespoon of olive oil
- 1 tablespoon of onion powder
- 1 tablespoon of salt
- 1 tablespoon of garlic powder
- 4 tablespoons of paprika
- 1 tablespoon of black pepper

Instructions

- Initially heat the oven to 400°F.
- The rub should be first blended together. Close the tenderloin of the pork in the olive oil, followed by the rub. The flat side should be put down in the middle of a baking pan of 9X13 in measurement.
- In a big bowl, mix the sage and vegetable with olive oil, white wine, apple cider vinegar, and salt. Place then round the pork in the baking pan.
- Mix the glaze/sauce and share into two while the vegetable and pork are getting roasted.
- Roast the vegetable and pork for about 30 minutes, and then turn the fat-side of the tenderloin up. Moisten the pork with sauce, mix the vegetables, and put back in the oven.
- Roast for extra 5-20 minutes, basting every 10 minutes with glaze. A thermometer put into the thickest side should read 63°C or 145°F.
- Bring out from the oven, brush with extra glaze then let it cool for 5 minutes before serving.
- The remaining sauce should be used in serving it.

POTATOES AND SAUSAGE WITH SUMMER VEGGIES

Ingredients:
- 4 tablespoon of oil
- 2 tablespoon of kosher salt
- fresh chopped pepper
- 1 yellow bell pepper, sliced 1-inch squares
- 2 halved lb baby red potatoes
- 14 oz Italian chicken sausage,1-inch thick in slices
- 2 sliced big onions
- 4-5 mashed cloves of garlic,
- 1/2 red diced bell pepper,1-inch squares in size
- 4 cups of quartered and half inch thick zucchini,
- 1 sliced orange bell pepper,
- 1 tablespoon of garlic powder
- 4 tablespoon of fresh rosemary (or other very fresh herbs like thyme)

Description:
- Put the potatoes and oil in a big and dip skillet that doesn't stick with a lid that fits tightly at a high heat, apply pepper, salt and garlic powder. When the skillet becomes hot and begins to sizzle, the heat should be reduced to low. It should be cooked for about 20 to 25 minutes with tight lid, the pan should be shaken frequently so as not to allow the potatoes get burn. Take down from heat and let it cool for five minutes without uncovering it, bring out the potatoes in a separate dish.
- The sausage should be added to the skillet and cooked on a level of medium low, stirring frequently till it gets brown but not thoroughly cooked for 10 minutes. Add some pinch of salt and pepper to the sliced vegetables. Also put in the garlic, rosemary, pepper, and onions into the skillet and mix together. Keep stirring frequently till it gets brown. Add the zucchini and cook for extra five minutes, mixing it while cooking till it is well cooked.
- Produces about 14 cups

RECIPE FOR QUICK TWO-POT SEARED PESTO CHICKEN

Ingredients
- 3 pints of divided cherry tomatoes
- 1 cup of tomato pesto
- Pepper and Salt, to make it tasty
- 2 cubed eggplant
- 4 tablespoons of olive oil
- 4 teaspoons of crushed garlic
- Parmesan cheese
- 2 cubes of medium zucchini
- 10 pieces of mozzarella cheese
- 1 cup marinara mush
- 2 pound of sliced chicken breasts
- 4 tablespoons of sliced fresh basil

Preparation
- First heat it in the oven at 350°F.
- Add olive oil into a big, skillet safe for the oven then warm with medium heat.
- Sauté zucchini and eggplant with garlic for about 2 to 3 minutes. Take off the heat immediately the vegetables soften.
- The cherry tomatoes should be poured unto skillet and mixed in tomato pesto that is sundried.
- Use pepper and salt to season the chicken strips on a cutting board, to taste. Then place the chicken strips on the blended vegetables, pushing them in fairly into give way for some vegetables to be at the top.
- Spread marinara sauce on top the chicken. Put the mozzarella cheese at the top then put the skillet inside the oven for up to 30 minutes till the chicken is well cooked.
- Bring it out from the oven then spray sliced basil and parmesan cheese that is freshly grated before it is served.

SINGLE SHEET PAN OF COOKED SALMON WITH GARLIC AND SPROUTS OF BRUSSELS

Ingredients

FOR THE BRUSSELS SPROUTS
- 1 teaspoon salt
- 4 pounds of Brussels sprouts, with trimmed edges
- 6 tablespoons of Olive Oil with STAR Garlic Flavor
- 1/2 teaspoon of fresh crushed pepper

FOR THE SALMON
- 2 tablespoon Olive Oil with STAR Garlic Flavor
- 4 pounds of skinned salmon fillet, sliced into 6 parts
- fresh ground pepper, to make it tasty
- 2 tablespoons of dried oregano
- 6 to 4 cloves of crushed garlic 2 teaspoon of salt

Instructions
- First heat in the oven for about 450F
- The baking sheet should be spayed and greased lightly.
- Mix olive oil, pepper, salt, together with trimmed brussels sprouts, inside a big mixing bowl.
- Transfer brussels sprouts to the baking sheet that was initially prepared, place in a single file and bake for about 15 minutes, turning it while cooking.
- Start preparing the salmon.
- Apply little olive oil on the salmon.
- Share into two and squeeze squashed garlic on every fillet.
- Apply pepper, salt and oregano to season it.
- Take out the baking sheet from the oven; turn the brussels sprouts around, forming 6 empty place to accommodate the salmon fillets.
- Put the salmon inside the open spots then bake for about 10 to 12 minutes or till it is well cooked.
- Take out from the oven; allow it to cool for two minutes then serve.

RECIPE FOR BALSAMIC CHICKEN WITH CHARD AND BARLEY

Ingredients
- 16 ounces of chicken thighs without skin and should be boneless
- 1 teaspoons of fresh thyme leaves
- 1/2 thinly sliced yellow onion,
- 1 teaspoon salt
- 4 sliced ounces of button mushrooms
- 1 ½ tablespoon of balsamic vinegar
- 1 tablespoon of olive oil
- 3 grounded garlic cloves,
- 3/4 cup pearled barley
- 2 (28-ounce) can chopped tomatoes
- 1 ½ cups Swiss chard, chopped

Preparation
- First heat up the oven to 350° F.
- Use thyme and salt to season the chicken
- Heat a big oven safe pot or Dutch oven with heat about medium-high heat. Pour in oild and shake to coat the base. Put garlic, mushrooms, and onions then cook for about five minutes till it becomes brown. Add vinegar and turn for one minute. Add barley, both tomatoes and juices and make them to simmer.
- Put the thighs of the chicken inside the pot and pour in water adequate enough to cover the chicken (1- 2 cups). Put them back to boil then put in the oven for about 20 minutes.
- Take away the pot from the oven and fold the chard in . Close the pot then come back after 15 minutes to the oven.

PEAS AND SHRIMPS ONE POT COUSCOUS

INGREDIENTS
- 2 tablespoon of olive oil
- 2 lb of deveined big shrimp, already peeled with the tails on
- 2 sliced small onion
- 2 sliced bell pepper,
- 6 minced cloves of garlic
- ½ cup of raisins
- 4 cups of good chicken broth
- 2 cup of couscous
- 2 tablespoon of cumin
- Garnish with parsley
- 2 tablespoon of paprika should be smoked
- Pepper and salt should be added to make it tasty
- ½ cup of sliced pistachios,
- 1 cup of peas already frozen

INSTRUCTIONS
- Add toss, pepper, salt, smoked paprika, and cumin to season the shrimp.
- The olive oil should be heated in a big skillet. Put in the shrimp when the oil becomes smoking hot then cook for 1 or 2 minutes till both sides become pink. Take out the shrimp from the skillet and keep it separate.
- Pour in the bell pepper and the sliced onion into the skillet then fry till the onion becomes shinny. Put in your raisins and garlic then cook for one more minute.
- Pour in the chicken broth and couscous into the skillet to boil, the off the heat. The couscous should be cooked for up to ten minutes till the whole chicken birth becomes absorbed. Pour in the frozen peas, and then cook it for some minutes till there is no more frozen pea.
- Add the shrimp then take the skillet off the heat. Parsley and pistachios should be used to garnish it.

RECIPE FOR MUSHROOM SOUP AND WILD RICE

Ingredients
- 2 cloves of grounded garlic,
- ½ large neatly sliced onion,
- 2 sliced celery stalks
- 1 ½ tablespoons of good olive oil
- 1 pounds of sliced blended mushrooms
- 2 sliced carrots
- ½ tablespoon thyme leaves, fresh preferably
- 2 cups of vegetable broth or water
- ½ cup of well stored white wine
- sea salt
- 1 ½ cups of brown or wild rice, cooked

Preparation
- Fry the celery, garlic, onion, and carrots with olive oil and around 1 teaspoon of salt in a big pot till it gets soft and not brown.
- Pour in the mushroom and thyme inside the oil to coat them with it. Pour in extra 1 spoon of salt, and then add little oil to lubricate the base of the pot after around two minutes, and then continue cooking the mushrooms.
- Pour in the vegetable broth or water to cook the rice when the juices start coming out of the mushrooms. Off the heat after it gets boiled. If the soup becomes thick feel free to put little water, then add adequate salt.
- Scoop into serving bowl, fresh thyme can be used to garnish it if you desire.

SRIRACHA & STEAK LETTUCE SHAWLS

INGREDIENTS
- for garnishing, green onions
- large sliced onion
- 2 lb of diced fajita strips,
- 6 cloves of diced garlic,
- 2 bell chopped pepper,
- other kind of lettuce leaves, romaine or big iceberg
- 4 tablespoons of coconut amino
- 4 tablespoons of sriracha
- sesame oil, a drizzle
- pea shoots, just few

INSTRUCTION
- Pour in oil into a pan and heat it till it becomes shimmery for about 1 minute.
- Add and toss your fajita meat which should be cooked at a high temperature for up to two minutes
- Include the peppers and onions and keep cooking at least five minutes, till it becomes brown turning it occasionally.
- Include the sesame oil, pea shoots, sriracha,, garlic, and coconut aminos
- Take down from the heat when the sauce is absorbed and the vegetables and steak becomes well coated.
- Scoop into cups and sprinkled with green onions already diced.
- To enjoy it serve when warm!

SMOKING HOT CHILI

INGREDIENTS
- **2** cloves grounded garlic,
- **3** slices bacon, maple-cured
- ½ teaspoon of paprika, smoked
- ¼ teaspoon of sea salt
- **1** red sliced onions,
- ¼ teaspoon crushed cumin
- ½ poblano sliced pepper,
- ¼ teaspoon of Greek oregano, dried
- ½ can of whole San Marzano tomatoes, 28-ounce cans, hand crushed
- **1 ½** espresso tablespoons, single shot
- Pepper, freshly ground
- ½ cup of freshly minced cilantro leaves
- ½ remade sliced chipotle pepper
- ½ jalapeno ground pepper,
- ½ cup of cream, sour
- **1** tablespoon undiluted maple syrup
- **1** cups of red kidney beans, cooked and drained
- **2** chopped scallions,
- **1** cups of black beans, cooked and drained

PREPARATION
- On a medium heat, cook the bacon in a big saucepan till it becomes crisp and golden, put it on a wire rack so that the excess grease would be drained. Ground the bacon and keep it separate.
- Put back the saucepan on medium heat then fry till golden the bacon fat, for about one or two minutes. Pour in the sea salt, chipotles, poblanos, smoke paprika, jalapenos, cumin, and onions. Fry for about eight minutes. Turn all in the tomatoes then include the maple syrup, many pepper, oregano, and espresso. Simmer the chili. Lower the heat and cook slightly closed for up to 45 minutes pour in the cilantro and beans and cook for extra 5 minutes, till everything becomes totally heated.
- Dish out the chili to bowls, the top can be spayed the scallions, crumbled bacon also with the sour cream.

FRENCH THIN ONION BROTH

Ingredients
- ½ tablespoon of sliced fresh thyme
- 1½ lbs of thingly chopped yellow onions, medium sized
- 3 cups of beef broth, reduced-sodium
- ½ tablespoon of black pepper
- 1 Bay leaves
- 1½ tablespoon of Stevia
- 2 slices of Swiss cheese, reduced-fat ⅔ oz each
- ½ Tablespoon of olive oil
- 2 slices of whole grain baguette,1 oz each

Preparation
- The oil should be heated on a medium heat in a big saucepan. The sugar and sliced onions should be added, and allow to cook for about 48-50 minutes, occasionally stirring it till they become golden of soft.
- Stir in the pepper and bay leaves and thyme in the broth. Allow it to boil at medium temperature. Bring it down to simmer open it and cook for about 30 minutes. Then take out the bay leaves.
- Put one cup of soup in for dishes which are broil-safe. The slices should be cut into cubes. Every bowl should have a bread cube covered with a slice of cheese. Stir rigorously for 1½ minutes, till the cheese becomes fairly brown or bubby. The bread slice should be kept whole if there are no dishes that are broil safe afterwards keep them on the baking sheet. The cheese slices should be broiled on it like that.

PARSNIP ROSEMARY AND GARLIC POTATO MASH

Ingredients
- 2 pound of baking potatoes
- For taste add black pepper
- 4 tablespoons of butter, unsalted
- 2 pound of maybe 1 big or 2 medium parsnips
- 4 teaspoons of ground fresh rosemary,
- ½ cup Silk® Original Almondmilk, Unsweetened
- 2 tablespoon of garlic, minced
- ½ tspn of salt

Direction
- The parsnips and potatoes should be peeled and sliced in pieces about 1- to 2-inch
- Pour them into a big saucepan then pour in enough water to cover them. Cook them till they become soft for up to 15-20 minutes.
- A little saucepan should be heated on a medium-low level.
- Pour in rosemary, garlic, and butter, then cook till the butter and garlic start getting brown, at least 3 minutes.
- Dry the parsnips and potatoes, and put them again into the pan used in cooking them.
- The almondmilk and butter mixture should be added to parsnips and potatoes, mash with a potatoes masher the way you want
- Add pepper and salt for seasoning

THIN PORK TACOS

Ingredients
- 3 pound of the tenderloin of a pork
- 2 tablespoon of fine brown sugar 6 cloves of minced garlic,
- 1 cup of water
- 2 jar tomato salsa (15-ounce) as you desire
- 2 tablespoon of fine chili powder
- 1 cup Mexican cheese, low-fat and shredded
- 2 tablespoon of cumin, well ground
- 2 teaspoon of fresh cayenne pepper
- 2 package of La Tortilla Factory Smart & Delicious Low-Carb
- 2 tablespoon of fresh jalapeño peppers
- 4 cups of shredded purple cabbage,
- 2 teaspoon of salt
- High Fiber Whole Wheat Tortillas,
- 2 sliced medium tomato,

Direction
- The pork tenderloin and water should be put on a slow cooker.
- Mix the brown sugar, garlic, jalapeno, chili powder, cumin, tomatoes salsa, cayenne pepper and salt then pour into the pot containing pork tenderloin.
- Cook at a low heat for about 8 hours and on a high heat for about 5 hours
- The pork tenderloin should be taken out of the slow cooker then torn apart with a fork. Pour back the torn pork tenderloin to the slow cooker again and cook for extra 15 minutes.
- Serve a cup of pork on warm tortillas with 2 tablespoons of tomatoes, shredded lettuce, and one tablespoon of cheese on every tortilla.

TWO PANS OF THAI QUINOA DISH WITH SPICY PEANUT AND CHICKEN SAUCE

Ingredients
- 4 cups of sliced chicken, precooked
- 2 Tablespoon of olive oil
- 6 minced garlic cloves,
- 2 small diced red onion,
- 4 cups of sliced broccoli,
- 1 cups of red cabbage, sliced
- 1 tsp minced ginger
- 3 tablespoon of salt
- 1 cups of carrots julienned
- 2 cup of washed and dried uncooked quinoa,
- 3 tablespoon pepper
- 4 cups of chicken stock
- 4 cups of frozen thawed edamame,

Peanut Sauce:
- 1 Tablespoon of honey
- 3 Tablespoon of water
- ¼ tablespoon of red pepper flakes
- ¼ cup of sliced Peanuts
- ¼ cup of peanut butter
- 3 Tablespoon of rice vinegar
- ¼ tablespoon of crushed ginger
- ⅛ tablespoon of sesame oil
- 1 Tablespoon of soy sauce, gluten free
- *To Garnish:*
- Cilantro just a Handful

Instructions

- Quinoa Bowl: the oil should be heated in a big skillet, on medium heat. Pour in the red onion and fry for at least 4 to 5 minutes and till it is soft. Pour in the ground garlic then cook till it fragrant.
- Pour in the carrots, cabbage and broccoli. Stir it and cook it for at least one minute.
- Pour in the ginger, chicken stock, pepper and salt, and quinoa. Stir thoroughly and cook it while closed for about 20 minutes.
- Take away the cover then botch. The chicken and the edamame should be added. Cook after stirring till the chicken becomes well heated for about 1 to 2 minutes.
- To Prepare the Peanut Sauce: While you are still cooking the quinoa, every ingredient for preparing the sauce should be mixed and stirred till it is totally smooth.
- To Serve: pour in the mixed quinoa; it can be topped with peanuts, cilantro, and peanut sauce.

FRESH QUINOA CORN POTAGE

Ingredients
- 1 cup of quinoa
- ¼ cup of good butter
- 1 medium sliced onion,
- ¼ cup of flour
- 1 chopped red pepper,
- 1 tsp ground garlic
- 3 cups of chicken broth
- 3 cups of quality milk
- 4 cups of fresh or frozen corn
- 1 can of dried and washed white kidney beans,
- 1 tablespoon of parsley, dried
- ½ tablespoon of thyme, dried
- 1½ tablespoon of salt
- Noncompulsory: to garnish add shredded cheese

Instructions
- The quinoa should be toasted in a big pot for on a medium heat at least 3 to 5 minutes.
- The butter should be melted in that particular pot. Pepper and onion should be added then fry on a heat that is medium high till it start becoming brown and soft. Put in the garlic and cook at maximum for a minute
- Stir the flour in it till it mixes well. Pour in the milk and broth one after the other then wait thrill the soup becomes a bit thicker before pouring in another cup.
- Add the thyme, parsley, salt quinoa and beans. Let it boil while frequently stirring it. The heat should be taken down to medium low or medium then simmer it without closing for about 15 to 20 minutes till the quinoa becomes well cooked, frequently stirring it.

TWO-PANS OF CHICKEN BURRITO DISHES

Ingredients
- guacamole 5 cups of chicken broth, low-sodium
- 6 tablespoon of olive oil
- 2 pound of sliced chicken breast without bones
- ½ cup yellow onion, sliced
- 4 cups of cheddar cheese, monterey jack or colby jack
- 2 15oz can of washed and dried black beans
- green onions chopped
- 2 cup of rice uncooked and extra-long grain
- 1 teaspoon of chili powder
- freshly chopped tomatoes
- 2 14.5 oz can of drained chopped tomatoes
- 1 teaspoon of powdered garlic
- 2 teaspoons of fine cumin
- sour cream
- kosher pepper and salt

Instructions
- First fry the onions in an olive oil about 2 tbsn till the start getting soft.
- ½ spoon of black pepper and one spoon of kosher salt should be used to season the sliced chicken.
- The chicken should be placed in the pan and subsequently cooked on a heat about medium high in level till the chicken starts browning.
- The chicken should be moved to a section of the pan then pour extra tablespoon of olive oil then deep fry the uncooked rice till some grains begin to turn golden brown or at least two minutes.
- Stir in, canned tomatoes, black beans chicken broth, chili powder, cumin and garlic powder.
- Simmer, close and turn down heat to level low
- Cook for up to 20 minutes or till the rice becomes soft.
- Add the pepper and salt as season
- Spray cheese on it then close, then set off the hit for about 2 to 3 to make the cheese melt.
- Guacamole, sour cream, fresh tomatoes and green onions should be used to garnish it.

ENCHILADAS SKILLET OVEN DISH WITH SWEET POTATO

Ingredients
- 4 small sliced red chili peppers with its seeds taken out,
- 2 C RiceSelect Arborio Blend ™ with Jalapeño
- 2 diced medium zucchini, cored
- 4 oz cream cheese, low fat
- 4 peeled medium sweet potatoes, sliced
- 2 15oz can of dried and washed black beans,
- 1 C sweet corn, frozen
- ½ 4oz of slice green chilis, canned
- Garnish with Cilantro
- 2 14.5oz can of sliced tomatoes and spicy red pepper
- 4 chipotle peppers with seeds taken out and sliced in adobo sauce
- 2 C shredded cheese, Mexican blend
- ½ C water
- 2 10oz can enchilada sauce of mild green chili
- 2 10oz can of red enchilada sauce
- 1 tablespoon of olive oil

Directions
- A big skillet should be heated on a medium high heat. Pour in little quantity of olive oil about 1/2 tablespoon as well as the sweet potatoes and deep fry for abouy2 minutes
- Add the chipotle peppers, red chili peppers, and zucchini, then cook for about 6 minutes.
- Turn down the heat to medium low and add in the rice. It should be cooked for at least one minute with frequent stirring. The water, enchilada sauces, diced tomatoes, black beans, and corn and diced green chilis. Mix properly and boil. Close then simmer for about 25-32 minutes, till the rice becomes soft.
- Immediately the rice cooking has been done in the 2oz of cream cheese. Spray the shredded cheese on it and broil till the cheese becomes bubbly. Cilantro can be used to garnish it if you wish.

WHITE BEAN, KALE, AND POTATO HASH (FREE FROM GLUTEN AND VEGAN)

Ingredents
- 2 big scrubbed russet potato, sliced into very little dice
- 4 Tablespoons. Ghee, Earth Balance, or Olive oil,
- ½ cup of thinly cut white onion,
- 2 can of dried and washed white beans, **Great Northern beans was what I used**
- 5 – 6 cups of ribbon like sliced Lacinato Kale **AKA:Dino Kale,**
- 2 zested lemon,
- 1/2 cup Parmesan cheese, shredded **if vegan then omit**
- Kosher black pepper and salt to give taste
- To taste add ground red pepper flakes

Procedure
- The Earth Balance should be melted in a thick bottomed skillet on medium-high heat. Adequate amount of Kosher salt and the potatoes should be added, stir properly to coat. Close the skillet with a very tight lid then cook for about 7 to 9 minutes, turning frequently to make sure there is browning on the both sides of the potatoes.
- The white beans, potatoes and the onions should be added to the skillet. It should be well mixed, the onions and beans should be properly arranged into one layer inside the pan and cooked for about 3 to 5 minutes turning periodically to make sure the beans get brown and crisp.
- Pour in the kale ribbons and cook for a little while till the kale slightly wilts. Take down from the heat and spray the black pepper, salt, red pepper flakes, and lemon to make it tasty. Then serve.

CHANAMOOSALA

Ingredients
- 4 tablespoon of vegetable oil
- 4 minced medium onions,
- 2 minced clove garlic,
- 4 teaspoons fresh ginger, grated
- 2 fresh, hot minced green chili pepper,
- 2 tablespoon coriander, ground
- 4 teaspoons cumin, ground
- 1 teaspoon crushed cayenne pepper
- 2 teaspoon turmeric, ground
- 4 teaspoons of toasted and blended cumin seeds,
- 2 tablespoon of amchoor powder
- 4 teaspoons of paprika
- 2 teaspoon of garam masala
- 4 cups of tomatoes, cut to pieces or 2 15-ounce can of thinly sliced whole tomatoes and their juices,
- ½ cup of water
- 8 cups of chickpeas, cooked or 2 cans of chickpeas, (15-ounce), dried and washed
- 1 teaspoon of salt
- 1 of lemon juice

Method
- The oil should be heated on a big skillet, pepper, ginger, and garlic should be added and fried on medium heattill it becomes brown. The heat should be lowered to medium low and the turmeric, coriander, cumin seeds, cumin. Paprika, garam masala and amchoor. The mixture of the onion should be cooked for 4 minutes, and then any other juice together with the tomatoes should be added. Chickpeas and water should be added too. Open it and simmer for about 15 minutes, then turn in lemon juice and salt
- Could be eaten immediately or reheated when desired. This kind of curries reheats properly.

35-MINUTE ZITI, SKILLET SEARED

Ingredients

- 2 lb de-cased from hot Italian sausage,
- 2 (14.5-oz) can sliced tomatoes tomatoes and garlic, fire roasted
- 2 (8-oz) of can tomato sauce
- 1 (6-oz) of can tomato paste
- 2 Tablespoon of Italian seasoning, dried
- 32 oz ricotta cheese, whole milk
- 8 oz parmesan cheese, fresh grated
- 2 tablespoon of salt
- 2 tablespoon of black pepper
- 2 lb of dry pasta
- 6 cups of water
- 2 (8-oz) of package sliced Italian cheese blend
- To garnish add basil

Preparation

- In a big skillet of about (12-inch) on high heat the brown sausage, for 20 minutes. Pour in the Italian seasoning, water, dried pasta, and tomatoes sauce. Turn and mix then let it boil till the pasta is dente
- At the same time mix the ricotta, salt, pepper, and parmesan cheese into a bowl.
- Make the ricotta mixture into pasta. First heat the oven to make it boil. Shredded cheese can be used as toppings for the skillet and put into the oven. Broil till the cheese becomes golden brown and bubbly. Watch it closely till you have a crispy cheese.
- Use basil to garnish. Serve and have a good meal!

SIMPLE SUMMER DISH: TWO-PAN STRAWBERRY SHORTCAKE, CHICKEN MANY MORE

Ingridents
- 7 un-skinned chicken drumsticks
- 7 roughly sliced thick bacon or strips pancetta,
- Canola oil for sautéing, or other types of neutral oil
- 4 cups unevenly cut fresh herbs like parsley, basil, celery leaves too, tarragon or cilantro
- 2 tablespoon of butter unsalted
- 6 peeled garlic, whole cloves
- 2 sliced white onion,
- 4 seeded jalapeño peppers, roughly sliced
- 10 cups of homemade chicken stock, can be bought in stores too
- 4 cups of Arborio rice
- 2 cup fresh shelled peas,
- Little Olive oil, to drizzle

Direction
- The oven should be first heated to 350 degrees. Pour in canola oil in a pot that is oven proof, on a medium heat. Put the chicken inside and fry till it becomes golden brown and properly seared. Take out the chicken and place separately.

- The heat should be turned down to medium then pour in the bacon or pancetta, jalapeno, onion, and garlic. It should be cooked for about 12 minutes, turning it occasionally to prevent the ingredient from getting burnt or sticking at the bottom of the skillet. Pour in your rice and keep turning for up to 10 minutes.

TWO PLATES OF MUNG BEAN DISH

Ingredients
- 1 cup of mung beans, sprouted
- 3 cups of broth or water
- 4 sliced green onions, pale and white arrears alone
- 2 trimmed ribs celery, cut into c-shapes
- 1 diced apple,
- 1 sliced avocado, ripe
- 1/3 cup of sliced almonds
- 1/4 cup of olive oil
- 3 tablespoons of sliced Italian parsley, packed loosely
- 2 tbsp of lemon juice
- Add freshly crushed black pepper and sea salt to taste

Preparation
- Boil the water in a saucepan of medium size. Pour in the mung beans and boil gently for about 10 minutes. Take out the pan from the heat. Close it and let it remain still for about 8 to 16 minutes till it gets to your preference. Take out the water.
- The green onions should be mixed with mung beans, apple, olive oil, celery, parsley, avocado, pepper, salt, and lemon juice. Turn properly. Share into eight bowls then serve.

THE 30 MINUTES FINAL THREE-CHEESE LASAGNA BROTH

Ingredients
- ¼ tablespoon of black pepper
- 15 oz ground hot Italian sausage,
- ¼ can tomato cream(6-oz)
- ½ diced can tomatoes and garlic, fire roasted (14.5-oz)
- ¼ Tablespoon of Italian seasoning, dried
- 4 oz of bell shaped campanelle, pasta dried
- ½ can tomato sauce (8-oz)
- 1 Tablespoon of Parmesan cheese, grated
- 1 chopped basil leaves
- ¼ tablespoon of onion powder
- 3 cups chicken soup
- ¼ tablespoon of kosher salt
- ¼ cup of ricotta cheese, part-skim
- 2 oz of mozzarella cheese, well shredded

Preparations
- Place on high heat a big pot(12 quart) in around five minutes, brown sausage. Ad little quantity of chicken soup if the dryness of the pot becomes too much.
- The remaining ingredients should be prepared
- Immediately the sausage becomes well-cooked add the sauce, onion powder, pepper, salt, tomatoes, seasoning then stir properly. Close and allow it to boil for up to 5 or 8 minutes.
- The pasta should be added and boiled then open it till it becomes dente for about 7 to 9 minutes. Put off the heat. Pour in the parmesan cheese, ricotta as well as the ½ mozzarella. Then stir properly.
- Serve each bowl with part of the remaining basil and cheese as toppings! Have a nice meal.

15 MINUTE WHOLLY LOADED POTATO SOUP: CHEESY BAKED

Ingredients
- 3 Tablespoon of flour (all-purpose)
- 3Tablespoon of unsalted butter
- sliced chives
- 4 cups of chicken soup
- 3 oz of cream cheese
- 2 oz mild of cheddar cheese, well shredded
- 1 cup of cream, sour
- 2 lb of precooked baked potatoes,
- 1 tablespoon of kosher salt
- 6 oz sharp white cheddar cheese, well shredded
- 4 slices of precooked and crushed bacon, thick crushed
- 1 tablespoon of black pepper

Instructions
- Warm a big stock pot on medium high level of heat. Butter should be added to the pot, whisk in the flour immediately the butter starts melting.
- Whisk properly and pour in the chicken soup gently, keep whisking add the cream cheese and sour cream, whisk till it all mixes well.
- Put a sliced potato with insides taken out into the pot.
- A potatoes masher should be used in smashing all the potatoes till it becomes the way you want put salt, pepper, and sharp cheddar. Stir well till the whole cheese is well melted.
- Serve and have a nice meal!

BROCCOLI WITH CHEESE & MAC

Ingredients
- 1 tablespoon of chipotle chile pepper, dried
- 4 Tablespoon of flour (all-purpose)
- ½ cup of unsalted butter, (8 Tbsp)
- 1 tablespoon of kosher salt
- 4 Tablespoon + 6 cups of whole milk
- 1 tablespoon of fresh black pepper, well ground
- 16 oz elbow macaroni, dried
- 24 oz of mild cheddar cheese, well shredded
- 4 cups of frozen broccoli florets

Preparation
- Add chipotle pepper, salt, pepper and butter into a big skillet on a medium high heat. Stir properly to mix well, add milk about 5 cups then close the skillet
- Add the macaroni immediately the milk begins to bubble, then allow the bubbling to continue for about 5 to 6 minutes till the pasta becomes well cooked, still occasionally stirring it.
- Pour in the broccoli then stir to mix well. Allow for three minutes to bubble
- Form slurry inside a resealable jar, mix 4 tablespoons of flour with 4 tablespoons of milk, and shake to mix well.
- To broil, preheat oven. Add chese about 16 ounces, then stir well o mix. The remaining ounces of cheese should be sprinkled on it. Put in the broiler for about 408 minutes till the cheese becomes golden browned or melted.
- Serve and have a nice meal!

HALF SKILLET OF CHICKEN POT PIE IN ONLY 20 MINUTES

Ingredients
- 1½ Tablespoon of butter, unsalted
- ½ lb of chicken breast, skinless and boneless, chopped to pieces
- 1/3 tablespoon of black pepper
- 1/3 table spoon of kosher salt
- ¼ cup flour (all-purpose)
- 1½ cups of chicken stock
- 1 cups of frozen vegetables, (carrots, peas and corn)
- 1 ½ oz fresh grated Parmesan cheese,
- ½ tablespoon of parsley, dried

Cheesy Drop Biscuits:
- 1 oz of fresh grated Parmesan cheese
- ½ Tablespoon of granulated sugar
- ¼ cup of melted butter, unsalted
- 1 cups flour (all-purpose)
- ½ cup of whole milk
- ½ Tablespoon of baking powder
- 1 teaspoon of kosher salt

Directions
- The oven should be preheated to 450°F.
- The butter should be melted in a skillet that is oven (10-inch) on a heat level that is medium high. Put the chicken then sprinkle pepper and salt, cooking till the chicken becomes brown turning both sides occasionally
- The flour should be added and whisked properly to mix. Add the cheese and vegetables, stir to mix well. The heat should be lowered to medium level. Let the mixture boil.
- Also mix baking powder, salt, sugar, cheese, and flour in a big mixing bowl. Add milk and butter to mix.
- Biscuit should be placed on the pot pie. Also place the skillet on the cookie sheet then push inside the oven to bake for about 8 to 10 minutes till the biscuit become golden brown.
- Spray fresh parsley on it, serve and have a nice meal.

MELISSA CLARK'S BAKED SHRIMP AND BROCCOLI

Ingredients
- 4 pounds of fresh broccoli, sliced into small sizes
- 8 tbsp of extra virgin olive oil (1/4 cup)
- 1 teaspoon crushed, or 1 teaspoon of whole coriander seeds
- 1 teaspoon crushed or 1 teaspoon of whole cumin seeds
- 3 tspn of kosher salt
- 2 teaspoon black pepper, freshly crushed
- hot chili powder about 1/8 teaspoon
- 2 pound of already shelled big shrimp, deveined
- 2 ½ teaspoons of lemon zest
- To serve, lemon wedges

Preparation
- The oven should be preheated to about 425 degrees. Pour in 4 tablespoons of oil, cumin, broccoli, coriander, chili powder, 1 teaspoon of pepper, and 2teaspoons of salt in another bowl mix the remaining 4 tablespoons of oil, the remaining 1 teaspoon of salt, the remaining 1 teaspoon of pepper, lemon zest, and shrimp.
- The broccoli should be spread in one layer on one baking sheet. It should be roasted for about 10 minutes. Pour in the shrimp into the baking sheet then mix with the broccoli. Keep roasting occasionally turning the sides till the shrimp become opaque and the broccoli becomes soft with golden edges. For up to 16 minutes or longer. It should be served with lemon wedges, also you can squeeze the lemon juice on all the broccoli and shrimp immediately before it is served.

35 MINUTE CHICKEN AND BACON BEER CHEESE BROTH

Ingredients
- 2 pound of boneless chicken breast without skin
- 12 slices of bacon, thick cut
- 2 cup of chicken soup
- ½ cup of butter
- 4 teaspoons of garlic powder
- ½ cup of flour
- 1 to 2 teaspoons of chile de arbol (ground to taste)
- 2 teaspoon of pepper
- Croutons
- 2 teaspoon of paprika smoked
- 16 ounces of shredded mild cheddar cheese,
- 2 teaspoon of kosher salt
- 2 cup beer, wheat beer (Belgian style Blue Moon)
- Chives
- 4 cups of half and half
- 2 teaspoon of Worcestershire sauce

Methods
- A 16 quart pot should be heated on a high level of heat. The bacon should be cut into the pot with a neat scissors. The bacon should be cooked till it becomes fairly crisp, while occasionally stirring it.
- Cut the chicken to small pieces.
- The bacon should be transferred from the pan into a plate. Pour the chicken into the bacon oil and cook. Occasionally stir it till the chicken is properly cooked. Transfer the chicken and bacon into a plate.
- Slice the butter into 2 spoon pieces and add the pan drippings. Add the spices and flour. Add the half and half, broth and beer. Turn properly to cause a bubble. Cheese whisk should be added to mix, turn till the mixture becomes smooth. Pour in the bacon, chicken and the Worcestershire sauce. Stir to mix well.
- Let it simmer till it is set for serving, occasionally stirring it.
- Croutons and chives should be used to garnish it. Have a nice meal!

ON THE STOVE CHEESE AND WHITE MACARONI

Ingredients
- 16 oz of shredded cheddar cheese, sharp white
- ¼ teaspoon cayenne pepper
- 32 oz box of original macaroni, prepared following the directions
- ½ teaspoon of white pepper
- 1 ½ tablespoon of flour
- 16 oz of shredded provolone cheese,
- ½ teaspoon of Dijon mustard
- ½ tablespoon of salt
- 1 cup of grated parmesan cheese
- 1 ½ tablespoon of butter
- 1 cups of milk

Methods
- Melt the butter in a big pot on low heat; add flour the stir to mix well. Cook for one minute stirring occasionally then pour in the milk and mix till it is smooth. Cook on low heat till it thickens, this should be about5-10 minutes. Add salt, cayenne pepper, parmesan, provolone, mustard and cheddar then stir till everything melts. The pasta should be added to the sauce then cook for extra 2 minutes. Bring down from the heat and let it rest for about five minutes to allow the sauce thicken well. Enjoy your meal!

TWO-SKILLET ENCHILADA PASTA

Ingredients
- green onions
- 4 cups of Colby Jack cheese, freshly shredded
- 4 cloves of ground garlic,
- low-sodium about 4 cups
- black olives
- 4 tablespoon of olive oil, extra virgin
- 1 of small bulb of sliced onion,
- 3 pounds of turkey meat, ground and seasoned with taco or 1.25 pounds of beef, thinly ground and 1 packet of taco seasoning, low in sodium.
- 16oz of rotini pasta, dried (around 4 1/2 cups)
- 2 19oz can of red enchilada sauce

Directions
- Sauté the onions and garlic in olive oil inside a big skillet with heat level on medium low till it becomes soft.
- Add the minced turkey meat the cook, till mat turns brown.
- Add the chicken soup, enchilada sauce, and pasta immediately the chicken has been well cooked.
- Allow it to get boiled then lower the heat and close the skillet.
- Cook with low heat, in a pan closed for about 30.
- Uncover and allow it to simmer for extra 10 minutes till the pasta becomes soft with reduced sauce.
- Take down from heat and turn in 2 cups of cheese.
- Extra cup of cheese should be used as toppings for the pasta then melt in a broiler for about 3 minutes then cover again to let the cheese melt due to the heat emanating from the pan.
- Green onions and black olives should be used to garnish it.

TORTELLINI

Ingredients
- 1 cups of Spinach
- 10 ounces of Cheese Tortellini
- 1 diced Tomatoes
- White Wine Marinade & 1 pack of Garlic, McCormick's Gourmet
- 2 cup of Asparagus, sliced into pieces about one inch
- 16 ounces of chicken broth or Veggie Broth
- 1 ½ cups of Water
- ½ cups of White Wine this is however optional
- 5 diced Basil Leaves
- ½ cups
- Water, if there is later need for it
- 2 dash
- Shredded Parmesan Cheese

Instruction
- Mix the ingredients together inside a slow cooker, put do not add tortellini
- Cook on a high level for 4 hours, or low for 5.
- The tortellini should be put inside at the final hour
- Use parmesan cheese, shredded as toppings.

CHICKPEA BROTH WITH CHARD AND SHREDDED CHICKEN

Ingredients
- 4 tablespoons of lemon juice from one fine lemon
- 2 finely sliced medium onion, (around 1 ½ cups)
- 4 tablespoons of olive oil
- parmesan rind 2 pieces (this is optional)
- black pepper freshly ground and Kosher salt
- chicken breast 3 pounds (around 6 medium breasts)
- 2 bunch chard, with the ribs removed and sliced into ribbons about 2-inch (around 8 to 10 cups)
- 2 ground medium clove garlic, (around 2 tsp)
- 2 (15 ounce) dried and washed can chickpeas,
- 8 cups of chicken stew bought in stores or homemade, low sodium chicken

Preparation
- The oil should be heated inside a skillet about 12-inch on a medium heat till it begins to shimmer. Pour in the onions and put a little quantity of salt and cook till the onions get soft. The garlic should be included then cook and stir in occasionally till it fragrant for around 1 minute.
- The chickpeas, rind and stock, chard and chicken should be added then increase the heat to boil the water. Ensure the chicken and chard has become soft a bit then simmer and close. Cook till the chicken is well cooked for about 15 to 20 minutes. Take out the chicken then allow cool off a bit, then shred to pieces. Pour back into the soup.
- If you are using the parmesan take it out. Pour in the lemon juice, pepper, salt together with the seasoning to give taste. Big grated cheese should be used as topping. Serve at once with more cheese on the table.

SKILLET COOKED SPAGHETTI

Ingredients
- 1 lb of ground beef
- 3 c. of water
- 2 ¾ c. tomato juice
- 1 can tomato paste Contadina(6 oz)
- 2 Tablespoon crushed onion, dried
- 2 Tablespoon of chili powder
- 1 1/2 teaspoon of oregano
- 1 teaspoon of salt
- 1 teaspoon of sugar
- 1 teaspoon of garlic salt
- 1 package spaghetti (7 oz)
- 1/2 c. Parmesan cheese

Preparation
- Cook the ground beef in a skillet till it is no longer pink. Sieve out the grease of the hamburger.
- Add juice, water, seasoning and tomato paste then allow to boil
- Lower the heat then pour in the spaghetti. Close then simmer with heat at low level for 30 minutes, frequently stirring till the spaghetti is well cooked. Spray parmesan cheese then serve.

15-MINUTE TURKEY AND WHITE BEAN CHILI

Ingredients
- ½ sliced small onion, (around 3/4 cup)
- ½ tablespoon juice freshly squeezed from 1 lime
- 1 tablespoons of olive oil
- ½ seeded and sliced jalapeño pepper, (around 2 tablespoons)
- 1 cups of homemade low-sodium or chicken broth bought-store
- black pepper freshly ground and Kosher
- 1 crushed medium cloves garlic, (around 2 teaspoons)
- 1 seeded and sliced peppers, (around ¾ cup)
- ½ (15-oz) can drained cannellini beans ½ tablespoon of ground cumin
- ¼ cup of cilantro, remove the stems and roughly slice the leaves
- ½ tablespoon of oregano dried
- ½ pound of white turkey meat, ground
- ½ (4-oz) can green chilies, sliced

Preparation
- The oil should be heated, in a skillet of about 12-inch on a medium high level of heat. Till it starts shimmering. Pour in the onions, poblano peppers, little salt and jalapeno. Turn until it becomes soft; add the cumin, stirring, oregano and garlic till it fragrant around a minute longer.
- Pour in the turkey carefully crushing it and cook till it immediately loses its pink pigment, 2 to 3 minutes. Then add the chilies, beans and broth and allow simmering. Smash some beans with a masher to make the broth thick. Add pepper, and salt, to season it and leave it to cook till it gets thick for 5 to 7 minutes. After this stir in cilantro and the lime juice, then spoon into your serving bowls.

TOMATO BROTH AND MUSSELS IN CHORIZO

Ingredients

-
- 2 tablespoon of olive oil
- black pepper freshly ground and Kosher salt
- 2 thinly sliced medium red onion,
- 4 pounds of polished and debearded mussels,
- ½ pound of quartered Spanish chorizo, sliced into about 1/4 to 1/2-inch in lengths
- 4 medium thinly cut cloves garlic,
- 2 can whole peeled tomatoes(28-ounce)
- ½ cup of red wine
- For serving Italian bread, crusty

Preparation

- The olive oil should be heated in a skillet of about 12 inch on a heat level that is medium high till it shimmers. Pour in the chorizo then cook, stir till almost all fat is extracted and the edges begin to crisp, around 4 minutes. Pour the chorizo in a separate bowl.
- Pour the onions into the skillet, and then stir till it starts to soft in 7 to 9 minutes. The garlic should be added then cooked till fragrant, for extra 30 minutes, the pour in the tomatoes with their juices. Carefully use a potato masher or a wooden spoon to break the tomatoes, simmer, then add pepper and salt as seasoning and taste.
- Let the tomatoes cook till it is almost melted, but not thick, at least 8 minutes. Pour in the wine stir it also put in the mussels. Close and cook, shaking the pan once in a while, till almost all the mussels become open, for about 3 to 4 minutes. Stir in the chorizo and remove any of the mussels that is still unopened. Use crusty Italian bread to serve it.
  .

SWISS CHARD AND VEGGIE CITRUS PASTA

Ingredients
- 2 tablespoons of olive oil
- 1 bunch of trimmed Swiss chard with no stems, sliced into ribbons about 2-inch
- 1 big thinly sliced shallot, (around 3/4 cup)
- black pepper freshly ground and Kosher salt
- Touch of red chile flakes, dried
- 4 1/2 cups vegetable stock, homemade or purchased in stores and vegetable soup with-sodium
- 1 pound of fusilli pasta, whole wheat
- 2 tablespoons juice, fresh ones and 2 tablespoon of zest from lemon
- 1 tablespoon of sumac
- For grating, Parmigiano-Reggiano,

Preparation
- The oil should be heated in a skillet of about 12 inch size on a medium high heat till it begins to shimmer. Put in the chard stems and use pepper and salt to season. Also cook for about 5 minutes till it becomes soft, put in the shallots continue cooking till they get soft too. In about 4 minutes add the red chile flakes and little salt for around 4 minutes.

- The stock and the fusilli should be added to the pan, increase the heat and keep cooking following the directions till it remains about 4 minutes for the pasta to be ready. Then add the chard leaves also keep cooking till both pasta and chard are done. The zest and lemon juice should be stirred and seasoned the way you want. Share into plates, put cheese that are freshly grated and sumac on it.

ALLA CARBONARA KALE AND SKILLET SPAGHETTI

Ingredients
- 8 ounces of guanciale, bacon, or pancetta, or slice to pieces about 1/2-inch
- 1 thinly cut shallot, (around 1/4 cup)
- 3 cups of sliced curly kale, without stems, leaves sliced into ribbons about 2-inch
- Black pepper freshly crushed with Kosher salt
- 3 ½ cups chicken stock, homemade or low-sodium chicken soup bought in stores
- 1 pound of spaghetti
- 4 eggs
- 1 cup Parmigiano-Reggiano, freshly grated

Preparation
- The bacon should be heated in a skillet about 12 inch, occasionally stirring it till the fat melts properly and starts to crisp, around 4 minutes. Pour in the shallot then cook till it begins to scent and becomes a bit soft, around 1 minute. The kale should be added, continue cooking, and stirring till the kale is well cooked and crisp, this should be about 3 to 5 minutes. Pepper and salt should be added to season. Put the bacon, shallots and bacon in a separate bowl.

- The pasta and broth should be transferred into that same pot, increase the heat and boil, cook following the directions till it becomes dente, occasionally stirring it to make sure it doesn't stick. The raw cheese, black pepper, and eggs, should be added to the mixture of kale and bacon when the pasta is about getting done. Immediately the pasta is set take down from the heat, pour in the kale mixture into the pan the stir well with a spoon till it gets creamy and thick. Black pepper should be added as a seasoning and it should be served with cheese on one side

COOKED SHAKSHUKA

Ingredients
- 1 thinly cut medium onion, (around 1 cup)
- 5 tablespoons olive oil
- 1 (28-oz) can whole peeled tomatoes
- 3 medium crushed cloves of garlic, or grated using a microplane (around 1 tablespoon)
- 1 tablespoon of chili flakes, dried
- black pepper freshly ground and Kosher salt
- 5 to 6 eggs
- ½ cup of roughly sliced packed cilantro
- 1 crushed serrano pepper,
- 1 teaspoon of cumin
-

Preparation
- The oil should be heated in a skillet of about 12-inch on a medium heat level. The pepper and onion with little inch of salt should be added and stirred till they become soft. The chili, cumin, garlic, and flakes and stir it till it saints for about a minute. Tomatoes should be added wait for some minute for it to get warmed then make use of a potato masher to break them to pieces. The heat should be turned low and the meal left to cook and become thick. Pepper and salt should be added as seasoning for taste

- The egg should be broken carefully into the sauce, ensure they do not overlap by spacing them, the heat should be lowered close and let it cook till it reaches the wanted texture, for about 9 to 16 minutes. Spray cilantro on it and serve it with some warm pitas and crusty bread.

ONE POT ASPARAGUS AND BLACKBERRY GLAZED SALMON

Ingredients
- 2 pound tinny asparagus spears without thick end
- 2 tablespoon vinegar, red wine
- ½ cup of preserves or blackberry jam
- 8 6-ounce salmon pieces, skinless
- 2 cup of vegetable broth with low sodium
- ½ teaspoon of salt
- 2 tablespoon of olive oil
- 2 teaspoon of both cumin and smoked paprika

Preparation
- The broth should be put in a big skillet and simmered you can make use of skillet of about 12 inch. Place the asparagus inside the pan immediately the broth starts to simmer. The salmon fillets should be placed on the asparagus, then sprayed with little pepper and salt. Close and allow simmering for at least 15 minutes till almost the whole liquid is evaporated.
- The remaining ingredients should be stirred together while the meal is simmering. The skillet should be taken from the heat. The blackberry mixture should be scooped on the salmon. The skillet should be kept about 8 inches in the broiler for about 4 minutes, also till the glaze begins to bubble.
- It should be served at once.
.

THAI PARSLEY CHICKEN CASHEW SKILLET

Ingredients

- 2 clove of crushed garlic,
- 2 pound of sliced little chicken cubes,
- ⅔ cup roasted cashews, unsalted
- ½ cup red onion finely sliced
- 1 tablespoon of sweet chili sauce
- 3 tablespoons of coconut oil
- 2 tablespoon soy sauce, low sodium
- 2 tablespoon of fish sauce
- ½ cup packed of roughly cut lemon basil leaves,
- 1 tablespoon of brown sugar
- Splash of water
- 1 cup packed of roughly sliced Thai basil leaves,

Direction

- Heat coconut oil in a big skillet on a heat medium high in level.
- The onions and garlic immediately is hot. Cook for 2 minutes.
- Put the chicken and keep cooking till every side turn white.
- The soy sauce, brown sugar, water, water and fish sauce in a little bowl.
- The sauce should be mixed in the skillet together with the leaves of the basil.
- Stir properly mix and cook for at least 1 to 2 minutes till the sauce gets thick.
- The cashew should be added, stir to mix then the heat should be turned off.
- Cooked rice should be used to serve it.

CHICKEN SKILLET WITH SRIRACHA LIME

Ingredients
- 12 chicken thighs, should be boneless
- pepper & salt
- ½ cup Extra Virgin Olive Oil Spectrum Naturals®
- juice of 2 limes
- 1 sliced big onion,
- 3 tablespoon of sriracha
- Garnish with cilantro

Direction
- The chicken should be washed and drained. Pepper and salt should be used as seasoning.
- Mix the lime juice, onion slices, chicken thighs, and olive oil. Stir to cover, close and freeze for at least two hours.
- The oven should be preheated to 400 degrees.
- The chicken should be placed in a big skillet that is open proof and put the marinade /onion mixture on it.
- It should be baked for 25 minutes, broiled for about 10 minutes till it start getting brown and crisp at the top.
- Carry it down from the oven and use cilantro to garnish it.

STEAMED CHICKEN THIGHS WITH GARLIC AND TOMATOES

Ingredients
- 4 chicken thighs on bone, skin-on
- 1 tsp olive oil
- Salt
- 3 garlic cloves, roughly chopped
- 1 vidalia onion, thinly sliced
- 20 oz. canned chopped tomatoes
- 1 cup chicken stock
- 2 sprigs thyme

Preparation
- The chicken thigh should be washed and dried. Use salt to season both sides well. The big skillet should be heated with the olive oil in it. Immediately it is hot put the thighs. The two sides of the thigh should be browned for at list 7 minutes or crisp, then turn the other side. Take out the chicken separately into a plate.
- The heat should be reduced and everything taken out except the 2 spoons of olive oil inside the pan. Put the garlic, immediately it begins to brown, the onions should be added, then cook till it becomes a bit translucent, at least 7 minutes. The tomatoes and chicken stock should be added. Make use of a soon to remove the brown areas from the base of the pan. Allow the pan simmer and once it starts to bubble thyme should be added. The chicken thighs should be place inside the sauce. Close the pan and allow simmering for at least 30 minutes.
- It should be served with rice. GREAT texture.

VEGETARIAN CHEESY ENCHILADA SKILLET

Ingredients
- 2 15oz can of original black beans
- To make it tasty add a good quantity of salt
- 2 cups of green enchilada sauce
- 4 cups of rice, cooked
- 1 sliced onion
- 1 teaspoon of black pepper
- 2 chopped green or red bell pepper,
- 16 oz of shredded cheese, Mexican blend
- 2 teaspoon of chili powder
- 2 Tablespoon of Olive Oil
- To garnish it add cilantro
- 1 teaspoon of cumin
- 2 cups of red enchilada sauce

Preparation
- The olive oil should be poured into a big skillet then the bell pepper and onion should be added, it should be cooked for about 4 minutes on medium heat.
- The black pepper, cumin, and chili powder should be added. The enchilada sauce, black beans, rice and 2 cups of cheese should be stirred in.
- Pepper and salt should be added, and simmered for about 5 minutes.
- The extra cilantro and cheese can be added as toppings. Let the cheese properly melt, and then serve.

EGGPLANT WITH CHICKEN MEAL

Ingredients
- 2 cubed eggplant, medium-sized
- 2 tablespoon of extra-virgin olive oil
- 2 chopped onion,
- 6 cups of organic spinach, fresh
- 2 15 oz. can tomatoes, organic chopped
- Optional: 1 teaspoon of red pepper flakes
- 2 tablespoon of Italian seasoning
- 4 crushed cloves of garlic,
- 2 lb. organic chicken breasts, boneless
- Freshly crushed pepper and Himalayan sea salt
- 2 tablespoon of fresh basil
- 1 teaspoon of crushed garlic

Direction
- The garlic and oil should be heated in a big sauté pan, heat
- Add eggplant and sliced onion then cook for about 5 minutes, occasionally stirring it till the eggplant becomes a bit soft and onions translucent
- The chicken breast which are still uncooked should be cut to cubes, and put inside the pan
- Allow it to cook for about 9 to 13 minutes till the whole chicken is well cooked.
- The fresh spinach should be added mixed properly and left to cook till the wilting of the spinach
- The seasoning and chopped tomatoes should be added
- Mix properly and allow to simmer for about 7-10 minutes
- Taste and add spice to your desired taste

PEPPERS WITH STUFFED RICE -AND- BEANS

Ingredients
- chili gravy and 30 ounce chili beans
- 4 yellow, red, or green sweet peppers, medium size, canned
- 2 cup of converted rice, cooked
- 2 15 ounce of can tomato sauce
- 8 ounces of shredded Monterey cheese

Preparation
- The pepper should be deseed with the membranes and tops removed. Stir the 1 cup of cheese, rice, chili gravy and chili beans, then transfer it to the peppers. The tomato sauce should be poured into the base of a 5 or 6 quart slow cooker. The peppers should be placed too in the slow cooker.
- Close the pan, cook on low level of heat for up to 8 hour to 8 ½ hours or high heat for about 4 to 4 ½ hours.
- Pour the peppers into the serving dish, the tomato sauce should be poured on the peppers, spray the remaining cheese on it.

CANNELLINI &MEDITERRANEAN KALE SAUCE WITH FARRO

Ingredients

-
- 2 14 1/2 ounce of tomatoes, fire-roasted with no salt added
- 8 cups of chicken broth, low-sodium or vegetable broth, low-sodium
- 2 cup of rinsed farro, or kamut
- 4 carrots, medium sized shared lengthwise and delicately cut crosswise
- 2 cup roughly sliced onion (2 large)8 cloves of sliced garlic,
- 8cups of roughly sliced fresh Swiss chard or green kale
- 6 tablespoons of fresh lemon juice
- 1 teaspoon ground red pepper
- ½ teaspoon of salt
- Sliced fresh basil or parsley
- 2 cup of roughly cut celery (4 stalks)
- 15 ounce of canned cannellini beans, with no added salt (white kidney beans), washed and dried
- 1 cups of crushed feta cheese (4 ounces)

Preparation

- Mix the tomatoes, carrots and celery, ground pepper, salt, faro, onion in a 6 1/2- or 4-quart slow cooker.
- Close the pot and cook over high level of heat for up to 2 hours, till the faro becomes soft but chewable. The lemon juice, beans and kale, should now be stirred in. close then cook for about 2 hours extra.
- Each serving should be sprinkled with basil, parsley or cheese.

SUMMERTIME SAUCE

Ingredients
- 3 1/2 cups of water
- 1 8 ounce of sliced fresh baby carrots, package peeled
- 2 tablespoons of sliced fresh oregano
- 1/2 16 ounce of diced red-skinned potatoes, package refrigerated rosemary-roasted seasoned with garlic as well as(about 4 cups)
- 2 17 ounce package cooked beef refrigerated or roast au jus
- 1 14 1/2 ounce can chopped tomatoes roasted with fire and garlic

Preparations
- The juice gotten from the roasted beef should be poured into the saucepan, with the meat kept separately. 2 cups of water and the carrot should be added and stirred. The heat should be lowered simmered and closed for about 6 minutes. The remaining water should be poured in, tomatoes, 2 tablespoon of oregano, and potatoes, make it boil again, then close. Simmer for about 6 minutes till the vegetables become soft. Cut the beef to sizes, add the stew then heat again. Use salt to season.
- It should be poured inside shallow bowls; then add black pepper which freshly ground and oregano as toppings. Then serve.

THIN SIMIAN OATS COOKIES

Ingredients
- 6 whole bananas
- 4 cups of old made oats
- 2 Tablespoon of peanut butter, creamy and low-fats
- ½ cup of black chocolate chips
- ½ cup of natural apple sauce
- 1 Tablespoon of brown sugar
- 1 teaspoon of vanilla

Direction
- The oven should be pre heated to 350 degrees. Place 2 cookie sheets parchly or spray them with cooking spray that is nonsticky.
- The bananas should be mashed with the fork in a bowl of medium size. The remaining ingredient should be stirred in.
- Allow it to batter for about 25-30 minutes.
- Scoop with a teaspoon and keep the batter.
- Bake for about 20 minutes.

NO-SUGAR CHOCOLATE FUDGE

Ingredients
- 1 cup of (120g)coconut butter
- 2 bananas, over ripped
- scant 1/4 teaspoon of salt
- 2 tablespoon of original honey or maple syrup
- ½ cup of cocoa powder or cacao (40g)
- optional 1 teaspoon of cinnamon
- optional 1 teaspoon of pure vanilla extract

Instructions
Ensure you melt the coconut butter before making use of it. Mix all the ingredients inside a food processor. The fudge should be smoothening into a candy mold or container. Plastic containers are perfect for this as they allow you pop out the fudge. Freeze it for some minutes or longer at least about 15 to 20 minutes before eating.

POT CHICKEN GRUB MEIN

Ingredients
- 4 cooked and sliced chicken breasts
- 2 325g Spaghettini pasta (325g)
- 7 cups of chicken stew
- 1 cup of soy sauce
- 1 teaspoon of ground garlic
- 1 teaspoon of salt
- 2-4 of red pepper flakes (more if you like it spicy!)
- 6 cups frozen Asian vegetable mix
- ½ cup of jam, apricot
- To garnish it add green onions

Preparation
- Mix the spaghettini, garlic, soy sauce, frozen veggies, chicken, broth, salt, and the red pepper flakes. In a big pot
- Make it simmer on medium heat, occasionally stirring it. Lower the heat to medium, keep cooking for about 20 to 24 minutes, till the pasta is cooked and with absorbed liquid it is proper to have little liquid in the pan. The apricot jam should be stirred in. Use sliced green onions to garnish it

SPINACH RECIPE WITH FRESH PEA PASTA {FAST AND EASY!}

Ingredients
- 12 ounces of little pasta figures, like Orecchiette
- ½ - 1 cup of substantial cream
- 20 ounces of defrosted spinach
- 1 cup of defrosted peas
- 2 cup of parmesan cheese, grated
- Add ground nutmeg, pepper, and salt to make it tasty.

Direction
- Follow the directions when cooking the pasta till it becomes very dente. Dry and keep aside.
- The pot should be placed back on a heat of about medium height then add the spinach and cream. Make it boil, bring down from the heat them mix it properly in the cheese and peas. Add seasoning to make it tasty before adding the pasta.

RICE SKILLET AND CHIPOTLE BLACK BEAN

Ingredients
- 2 tablespoonful of oil
- 1/2 diced, medium onion
- 2 cups of cooked brown rice
- 1/3 lime juice
- Water, 1/2 cup
- 1/2 teaspoon of powdered Chipotle (see below)
- 2/3 cup of properly drained and rinsed black beans
- Spinach, about 3-4 fistfuls
- Cilantro, about 3/4 cup
- 2 ounces of cheese (goat origin)
- 2-3 medium eggs
- Avocado, for garnishing

Method
- Heat olive oil over average heat in an 8" cast iron skillet. Afterwards, pour some onions and allow to cook for about 7-8 minutes.
- Sequentially, pour the black beans, chipotle powder, rice, lime juice, and water. Stir continuously while cooking till the rice and black beans are heated.
- After step 2 above, add cilantro and spinach, making sure to stir the broth until the spinach appears limp.
- Dig a hollow at the middle of the skillet into which cracked eggs will be poured. Add a sprinkling of goat cheese on top, cover, and allow to cook until the albumen are hardened and the yolk is set at an acceptable level. This could take around 8-13 minutes.
- Garnish with a sprinkling of cilantro and serve.

TWO POTS OF FRIED MEXICAN CHICKEN, WITH PALEO

Ingredients
- Virgin olive oil, 2 teaspoonfuls
- 3 lean, unskinned breasts of chicken, minced into 3" pieces
- 3 paprikas
- Broccoli flowerets, 2 cupfuls
- Cumin, $1^{1/2}$ teaspoonful
- 1 teaspoonful of chili pepper
- Bell pepper (smoke-dried), 1 teaspoonful
- 1 teaspoonful of pulverized cayenne pepper (discretional)

Instructions
- Place a big cooking pan on average to high heat, and allow it to get warm.
- Pour some oil and bring the oil to heat until it glimmers. This should take around 30 seconds.
- Incorporate the minced chicken, and allow to cook until it is evenly brown, all the while stirring intermittently. This should take around 8 minutes.
- Include the broccoli and peppers and allow to heat till they are fairly golden and tender. This should last for 12 minutes.
- Pour a small quantity of water and then add the spices. This will help to integrate the spices into the ingredients. The spice should be added with discretion; about 3 tablespoonfuls should suffice.
- Allow the ingredients to cook until the water has dried totally.
- The food is ready to be served!

SHRIMP IN SALT AND PEPPER

Ingredients
- 2 ounces of previously peeled and deveined shrimp
- Virgin olive oil, 2 tablespoonfuls
- 1/2 cup of minced garlic
- 3 teaspoons of branded Celtic sea salt
- Grinded fresh black pepper, 3 teaspoons

Instructions
- Place a big nonstick cooking pan on average to high heat, and allow it to get warm to pre-smoking levels.
- Pour some oil into the pan, heating the oil until it is glimmery. This should take about 40 seconds.
- Incorporate the shrimp and stir intermittently.
- Pour the pepper, salt and garlic.
- Flip the shrimp in the pan until it is evenly white. Be careful not to cook beyond necessary.
- Add a topping of vegetables, salad, rice, or place it in a taco!

TUSCAN PORK SLICES

Ingredients
- 6 pieces of lean pork chops
- 2 tablespoons of oil (butter, coconut, ghee, olive)
- 7 minced garlic cloves
- 3 cups of tomatoes, fresh and minced (if the tomatoes are not firm enough, you may include the liquid produced from cutting the tomatoes)
- 2 big bulbs of onions, minced
- 3 teaspoons of marjoram
- 2 teaspoons of dried sage
- 2 teaspoons of sweet basil

Instructions
- Place a big cooking pan on high heat till it gets warm.
- Pour some oil and allow to heat till it is glimmery. Care should be taken not to overheat the oil till it starts to smoke or burn. This should take around 30 seconds.
- Add the pork chops and allow to brown evenly on the two sides. Each side of the pork chops would require around 2 minutes.
- Before adding onions, decrease the heat to average to low levels.
- Each side of the pork chops should fry for 3 minutes before it is tossed. The onions should be stirred.
- Incorporate the garlic, seasoning and tomatoes.
- Boil slowly till the tomatoes are tender and the sauce is done. This should take around 6-7 minutes.
- Serve with zucchini noodles or alongside some pasta.

ANCIENT ASIAN STIRRED FRIED CHICKEN

Ingredients
- 3 tablespoons of coconut oil or olive oil
- 3 big breasts of chicken, minced into cubes of 1"
- 2 paprikas of whichever color
- 2 properly minced big white onions
- 2 courgettes, preferably minced into tiny pieces (or 6 small courgettes, as illustrated)
- 2 tablespoons of sauce; coconut aminos
- Sriracha , 2 tablespoons (actually, begin with 1 tablespoon and increase the quantity with discretion until you are satisfied with the flavor- it's savory!)
- A smattering of pea shoots

Instructions
- Pour and heat some oil in a heavy cast iron pan, until the oil glimmers.
- Regulate heat to average high, and place chicken in the pan and allow to cook till it is fairly brown. This should take around 7 minutes.
- Pour the peppers and onions. They should cook till they are fairly brown. This should take around 6 minutes.
- Pour the courgettes and allow to cook until all the ingredients are evenly brown. This should take around 8 minutes.
- Pour the coconut aminos and stir properly.
- Gradually, pour the sriracha sauce till you arrive at an acceptable level of heat. This heat level increases unnoticed, therefore ensure to pour it gradually. The quantity can be increased but without reversal. Take care not to pour excess.
- While the pan is still on the stove, add the pea shoots, and flip the ingredients until the pea shoots begin to become tender. This should take around 4 minutes.
- Bring the pan down from heat, and you can begin to eat!
- It can be placed in a lettuce wrap or eaten exactly as it is.

PALEO CRANBERRY AND ZUCCHINI PINE NUT PASTA

Ingredients
- 6 washed zucchinis,(with their tops removed)
- Pine nuts, 1 cup
- 3 tablespoons of coconut oil, ghee, olive oil, and walnut oil
- ½ cup of cranberries (fresh)
- For seasoning, Celtic sea salt

Instructions
- Make strands of zucchini with a vegetable slicer.
- Gently toast the pine nuts In a pan of small size.
- After making strands of zucchini, put it in a pan of high heat containing olive oil.
- Fry quickly for about 7 minutes on average high heat till the zucchini begins to turn brown.
- Put the cranberries and pine nuts.
- For 7-12 minutes, sautee the mixture until the cranberries appear to almost pop open and the zucchini is tender.
- You can serve it warm as a delectable main dish or a side salad.

PEPPERS STUFFED PALEO AND CHORIZO

Ingredients
- 7 seedless bell peppers with tops cut off (any color goes), remove the stem (for filling) and mince the tops.
- Chicken chorizo, 2 pound2
- 2 pounds of beef chorizo with fat trimmed
- 2 big onions
- 3 quartered then thinly sliced zucchinis
- Smoked paprika powder, 3 tablespoons
- Cumin, 3 tablespoons
- Powdered curry (red), 2 tablespoon
- Turmeric seasoning, 2 tablespoons
- Red pepper flakes and cayenne (optional) for spicing

Instructions
- Brown chorizo in a cast iron pan (or heavy pan).
- After the chorizo is properly browned, put the zucchini, minced pepper tops and diced onions to mix.
- Cook till the veggies turn brown.
- Get a taste of the mixture.
- If not tasty enough, put more spices and stir. The chorizo will most likely give oil in adequate quantity to necessitate the combination of spices and liquid. Otherwise, put a small quantity of water or olive oil.
- Taste the mixture and put more spices to suit your taste.
- Put the peppers, but ensure it is In a slow cooker.
- Cover up to 1" of the slow cooker with water.
- Incorporate the veggie mix and meat to the peppers with discretion.
- For 3 hours, cook on high heat till the peppers are tender.
- Bring down the pan and serve.

JICAMA HASH PALEO

Ingredients
- Ghee or butter, 3 tablespoons
- 2 big roots of jicama (peeled)
- 2 peeled big onions, cut in two and shredded into strips lengthwise
- 3 seeded bell peppers, cut in two seeded and shredded into strips lengthwise
- Fajita meat, 2 pounds
- 2 tablespoons of home-made, gluten-free montreal steak seasoning

Instructions
- Melt butter in a big nonstick cooking pan.
- With either mandolin, vegetable slicer or veggie slicer, shred jicama into spirals.
- Put the jicama in the pan and cook till it turns brown. This should take around 12 minutes.
- Bring down the pan and keep the jicama aside.
- Put the onions, peppers and fajita meat.
- Allow to cook till the mixture is well browned and the meat is properly cooked. This should take around 13 minutes.
- Put the jicama into the pan again and stir properly. Allow to cook for extra 7-12 minutes in order to release the flavors.
- Serve warm!

GREEN BEANS AND CRISPY FLESH CHICKEN BATONS (EASY & FOOLPROOF)

Ingredients:
- 4-8 drumsticks of chicken (the meat is better off when pulled straight from the bone and used in preparing salad the following day, so it's okay to make extras for leftovers)
- Olive oil, 3 tablespoons
- Butter, 2 tablespoons
- Any profile of seasoning you prefer out of pepper, salt, herbs de provence and rosemary
- Cooking pan (iron pan)
- Preheated oven of about 350 degrees

Method
- Melt oil and butter on the stovetop initially, and add seasoning to the chicken drumsticks. Make sure the drumsticks are dry.
- Fry the drumsticks in the pan till they are evenly brown, this should take around 4-6 minutes depending on the frying temperature.
- As soon as the chicken is browned (as stated in step 2), put the cast iron pan (with the chicken inside) in the oven and cook fully for 40 minutes at 350 degrees.
- Food is ready to be served!

SQUASH BOATS PALEO

Ingredients
- 2 halved and seedless spaghetti squash
- 6 minced garlic cloves
- Olive oil, 2 divided tablespoons

Instructions
- Divide the squash into two parts and remove the seeds with a spoon.
- Place squash in a cookie sheet, then pour some garlic and olive oil in it
- Place the mixture in the oven and bake for around 1 hour 15 minutes at 340 degrees until it is tender.
- To make a spaghetti texture, rake the tender squash with a fork. Remove the squash flesh from the shell.
- Season with pesto and stir.
- Personally, I prefer a topping of a bit of grated parmesan and red pepper flakes.

SQUASH PESTO PALEO

Ingredients
- 3 cups of basil leaves, fresh and packed
- 3 garlic cloves
- Pine nuts, ½ cup
- 1 cup (divided) of extra-virgin olive oil
- Ground pepper (fresh) and Kosher salt, for seasoning
- 1 cup of fresh Parmesan cheese, grated

Instructions
1. In a food processor, pulse the ingredients until they are at a desired texture.
2. Place the processed ingredients in an airtight container and refrigerate for about 5 days for storage.

SOLID BOILED EGGS

Ingredients:
- Eggs. The quantity is optional. It takes the same time to cook. Ensure the shells are not cracked.

Directions:
- Pour a cup of water into preferably the inner pot
- Put the steamer basket/trivet inside the inner pot
- Put the eggs Place the eggs on the steamer basket/trivet.
- Tightly seal the lid and also seal the vent valve unfailingly.
- On HIGH pressure select the option for "Manual" for any of these QR and finished yolks styles.
- Hard Boiled eggs – about 6 minutes
- Soft Boiled eggs – about 5 minutes
- Runny yolk eggs – (aka poached egg) – less than 2 minutes
- Following the QR, remove the eggs and put them in a bowl containing cold water. Once the water gets warm, change it to keep it cold. Once the eggs feel cold, put them in the refrigerator.

PROVENCE EGGS

Ingredients
- 8 eggs
- 1 (diced) medium onion
- 2 cups of cooked bacon or ham
- Heavy cream, 1 cup
- Kale leaves (diced), 2 cups
- Cheddar cheese, 2 cups (preferably *Dubliner Cheese* from grassfed milk; produced by Kerrygold's) (a subsidiary of Amazon)
- Herbes de Provence, 2 teaspoons
- Pepper and sea salt, ¼ teaspoon

Instructions
- Together with the heavy cream, whisk the eggs.
- Incorporate the other ingredients, ensuring to stir properly.
- Transfer the mixture to a dish (heatproof) and seal.
- To the instant pot, pour a cup of water.
- Put the steamer basket/trivet inside.
- Seal the lid and vent valve tightly.
- On HIGH pressure, select the option for "Manual" and cook for 25 minutes and NPR.
- Serve as soon as it's done.

STEAMED EGGS (KOREAN STYLE)

Ingredients:
- 2 big eggs
- Cold water, 1 cup
- Diced scallions
- A tinge of sesame seeds
- A tinge of pepper, salt and garlic powder

Instructions:
- In a small bowl, mix the water and egg.
- Over a fine mesh strainer, strain the egg mixture and put in a bowl (heatproof).
- Put the remaining ingredients, stir well and put it aside.
- To the inner pot of the instant pot, pour a cup of water.
- Put the steamer basket/trivet inside the pot.
- Put the egg mixture in a bowl and place the bowl in a steamer basket/trivet.
- Tightly seal the vent valve and lid of the pot.
- Set temperature to HIGH and select "Manual" setting for 7 minutes.
- QR after the timer goes off.
- Bring down and serve with hot rice immediately.

POTATOES BAKED IN THE INSTANT POT

Ingredients
- Potatoes – quantity based on your preference (not more than 6 pounds however). The potatoes should either be peeled or chopped based on preference. The potatoes should be of more or less equal size.

Instructions
- Into the steamer pot, place the steamer rack (contact the video for illustration)
- Pour into the instant pot, 1½ cups of water
- Incorporate the potatoes
- Seal the pot lid and the vent valve
- Manually decrease the time to 8 minutes
- Allow pressure valve release naturally upon completion of cooking (this should take around 24minutes)
- Food is ready, open lid to eat the potatoes!

INSTANT POT WHOLE CHICKEN

Ingredients
- Whole chicken, 2
- Desired seasonings
- Water, 2 cups
- 2 tablespoons of fresh coconut oil

Directions
- Put steam rack inside the instant pot, and pour 2 cups of water inside the instant pot.
- Heat the oil in a big skillet.
- Add seasonings to the chicken, then put the chicken in the oil, allowing the skin to scorch on its sides. Afterwards, withdraw from the heat.
- Put the Instant Pot contining the chicken inside the steam rack.
- Tighten the lid before setting Instant Pot (with the chicken) to chicken at high pressure. The time should be adjusted thus; 7 minutes per pound of chicken plus 3 minutes to the entire time. For example: 4 pounds of chicken would be 4×7=28+3+20 minutes.
- The chicken should be made to release steam while still in the pot for about 18 minutes. The chicken can be left in the pot a bit longer, but not more than 40 minutes (my recommendation).

PRESSURE COOKER RECIPE - AMARETTI STUFFED PEACHES

Ingredients:
- 2 cups of water (or red wine)
- Sugar, 6 tablespoons
- 1½ cups of crumbled Amaretti Cookies, crumbled (around 12 cookies)
- Almonds, 3 tablespoons
- 3 tablespoons of melted butter or olive oil
- Lemon zest, 2 teaspoons
- 5 mature but firm peaches

Instructions:
- Position the steamer basket, then pour sugar and wine into the pressure cooker to prepare the pressure cooker.
- Use a chopper to crush the almond and cookies. Afterwards, add the melted butter and lemon zest and mix.
- Thoroughly wash the peaches, cut them in two and take out the pit. Use a melon-baller to increase the size of the pit cavity.
- Use cookie crumble filling to fill the peaches, and dust the top of the peaches with same also. Afterwards, proceed to place the peaches into the pressure cooker's steamer basket.
- Close the pressure cooker and secure its lid. Set the heat to high and once the cooker is at pressure, reduce heat to minimum level necessary for cooker pressure to be maintained. Allow to cook at high pressure for 5 minutes.
- Upon completion, release pressure by opening the cooker.
- Use tongs to remove peaches to separate plates.
- Remove the lid, then decrease the red wine in the cooker until it has the consistency of syrup, then mizzle on the peaches.
- It is ready and can be served with vanilla ice cream or whipped.

OWL-SHAPE OATMEAL

Ingredients:
- 1 cup of rolled oats (certified and gluten-free)
- 2 cups of milk (nondairy)
- 2 sliced strawberry
- Few slices of almond
- 4 slices of banana
- 3 blueberries, dried
- Almonds, 2

Instructions:
- Boil the nondairy milk and oats together in a small saucepan. Simmer for 7 minutes on low heat, making sure to stir intermittently until the milk has been absorbed as desired.
- Serve oatmeal in a bowl of owl shape.

FOOD ART

Ingredients:
- Blueberries, a fistful
- Sweetcorn, a fistful
- Cheese (mini Babybel), 1
- 2 dried fruit strip Bear Yoyo

Method:
- Form the body of the blueberries by arranging them on a plate. For the straps, use the blueberries to form three lines. Use sweetcorn to design the arms and head.
- Halve the Babybel cheese as illustrated. To make strap, trim a part of the Bear yoyo as desired, then put it on top of the sweetcorn and use a topping of the halved Babybel cheese.
- Slice a small dot out of the Bear yoyo with the aid of a small-sized circle cutter, then proceed to finish the eye by adding it to the cheese. Cut out the mouth from a different piece of yoyo with the help of a fairly bigger circle cutter, then pop the cut part on top to get the shape of the mouth.

HEALTHY ENGLISH MUFFIN "DONUTS"

Ingredients:
- Muffins (English muffins)
- Cutter, circle hole-shaped
- Cheese (cream cheese)
- Coloring
- Sprinkles

Instructions:
- It's easy to prepare. Make holes at the middle of the English Muffins. Spread English muffins with cream cheese and use sprinkles to top. If you don't fancy plain cream cheese, you can color them with food coloring.
- Festive looking, aren't they! Can be eaten as lunch or served as a snack, with an accompanying fruit side.

THICK SPREAD AVOCADO

Ingredients:
- 3 cloves of garlic
- Garbanzo beans, 2 cans (30 ounces)
- Zest and lemon juice, 2 lemon
- Tahini, 3 tablespoons
- Avocados, 3
- Salt to taste
- Oil (olive oil)
- Ground bell pepper

Instructions
- Put garbanzo beans, zest and lemon juice, tahini, and cloves of garlic cloves tahini into a food processor. Blend till it attains a smooth consistency. Add some salt.
- After step 1, add the 3 avocados and allow the mixture to blend until it is fairly smooth. Once more, add a little salt to improve the taste. Transfer the contents of the processor to a bowl, then pour few tablespoons of olive oil atop the mixture, then add a sprinkling of ground bell pepper. Serve as desired; a few suggestions are with crackers or pita (chips or warm slices).

SPINACH DIP

Ingredients:
- Packaged frozen spinach, 2 (10 ounce each) melted, squeezed dry and emptied
- Mayonnaise, 1 cup
- Parmesan cheese, 1 cup (grated)
- Diced shallot, 3 tablespoons
- 2 diced garlic cloves
- Salt, 1 teaspoon
- Black pepper, 1 teaspoon (ground)
- Cayenne pepper, ½ teaspoon
- Greek yogurt, 1 cup

Instructions:
- Mix shallot, cayenne, mayonnaise, Parmesan cheese, salt, pepper, garlic, and chopped spinach in a big bowl until they have combined totally. Fold the Greek yogurt carefully into the mixture till it is fully incorporated. Cover the mixture bowl put in the refrigerator for not less than 1½ hours.
- You may choose to serve in a bowl alongside pretzels, tortilla chips, crackers or fresh vegetables, crackers, or serve in a bowl of bread alongside cubes of reserved bread. Excess dip after eating can be preserved for about 2 days by refrigerating it in an airtight container.

KICKOFF PIZZA

Ingredients:
- OSCAR MAYER Pepperoni, 30 slices
- Cheese pizza, 2 (12 inch each)
- Stripped KRAFT Singles, 2

Instructions:
- Pepperoni (OSCAR MAYER), 30 slices
- Cheese pizza, 2 (12 inch each)
- Stripped KRAFT Singles, 2

MEXICAN DIP (5-LAYER)

Ingredients:
Canned black beans (refried), 17 ounces
- Chili powder, 2 tablespoons
- Cumin, 1 teaspoon (ground)
- Sour cream (KNUDSEN) or BREAKSTONE, 2 cups
- KRAFT Cheddar Cheese (shredded), 2 cups
- 4 sliced green onions
- Black olives (sliced), 1 cup
- 2 chopped tomatoes

Instructions:
- Stir chili powder, cumin and beans into an 8-inch plate, making sure to spread the mixture in the plate's bottom.
- Pour layers of the other ingredients as topping.
- Store in a refrigerator for few hours.

CREAM PIE MINIS (BOSTON-STYLE)

Ingredients:
- Yellow cake mix, 2 packages (each, 2-layer size)
- JELL-O Instant Pudding (Vanilla Flavor), 2 packages
- Cold milk, 2 cups
- Whipped Topping (COOL WHIP),2 cups (divided)
- Semi-Sweet Chocolate (BAKER'S BRAND), 2 packages (4 ounces each)

Instructions:
- Firstly heat the oven to a temperature of 350ºF.
- According to the instructions on the package, prepare a batter (cake batter) and bake for 48 cupcakes. Allow to totally cool off.
- Use a whisk to beat the milk and pudding in an average-sized bowl for 3 minutes. Allow to stand for 7 minutes. For the meantime, halve cupcakes horizontally using a knife (serrated).
- Add a cup of COOL WHIP into pudding and whisk; use a spoon to place on the bottom halves of the cupcakes, use around 2 tablespoons for each. Proceed to cover the cupcake with cupcake tops.
- The remaining chocolate and COOL WHIP should be microwaved in a small-sized microwaveable bowl with temperature set at   HIGH for 2 minutes or less, or till appears to be virtually melted, stir at a 1 minute interval. Keep stirring until the chocolate is totally melted and the mixture is thoroughly blended. Allow to stand for about 20 minutes.
- Use the chocolate mixture to frost the cupcakes, and refrigerate for 20 minutes.

SUPER BOWL FOOD: MEATBALL SLIDERS

Ingredients:
- Frozen meatballs (melted), 12
- Marinara sauce, 1 cup
- Mozzarella or provolone (sliced), 4 ounces
- Butter, 1 tablespoon
- Powdered garlic, ¼ teaspoon
- Seasonings (Italian), ¼ teaspoon
- 4 hot dog buns or 12 dinner, cut in 3 places

Instructions
- Firstly heat oven to a temperature of about 400 degrees. Use foil to line pan (8X12) and spray the pan with cooking spray.
- In a saucepan, warm meatballs in marinara sauce over average heat. Hot dog buns should be separated from the dinner rolls, and then one saucy meatball should be placed on the bottom roll. Use provolone or mozzarella to top. Put the top roll on and slightly push it down. Put the slider (meatball slider) inside the pan and proceed to continue to put the rest of the sliders together.
- Place butter in a bowl and melt by microwaving. Pour the Italian seasonings and garlic powder and stir properly. Use the mixture of melted butter to brush the buns tops.
- Place in oven and toast for about 5-7 minutes or till it is toasted. I prefer the soft one that's not too toasty.

BUFFALO THICK SPREAD (HUMMUS)

Ingredients:
- Canned chickpeas, 2 (15 ounce each), rinsed and drained
- Garlic, 3 gloves
- Lemon juice from 1 lemon
- Pepper and salt, to taste
- Buffalo sauce, 3 tablespoons
- Extra-virgin olive oil, 3 tablespoons

Directions:
- With the exception of the olive oil, put all the other ingredients together in a food processor.
- Gradually pour in the oil while the processor is running
- Allow the ingredients to process they are creamy and smooth.

BAKED CHICKPEAS (BUFFALO)

Ingredients:
- Canned chickpeas, 2 (15 ounce each), rinsed, drained, and patted
- Buffalo sauce, 3 tablespoons
- Butter, 1 tablespoon
- Kosher salt, ½ teaspoon
- Garlic powder, ½ teaspoon
- Black pepper, ¼ teaspoon

Directions:
- Firstly heat oven to a temperature of 450F and apply grease to baking sheet.
- Melt butter, add it to the Buffalo sauce and stir in small-sized bowl.
- In a big bowl, pour the chickpeas, butter mixture and Buffalo sauce.
- Pour spices in the bowl and mix.
- Spread out (in one layer) the chickpeas on the baking sheet.
- Roast the mixture for about 18-24 minutes, making sure to shake the pan intermittently to avoid burning.
- Bring down from the oven once it is crispy and serve.

BREAKFAST SKILLET QUINOA

Ingredients:
- Thick-cut bacon (chopped), 6 slices
- Small sweet potato (chopped), 2
- Diced red onion, 1
- Diced red pepper, 1
- Diced green pepper, 1
- Sliced and diced mushrooms, 1 cup
- Diced cloves of garlic, 1
- Rinsed, uncooked quinoa, 1 cup
- Vegetable (low-sodium), 2 cups or water (or chicken stock)
- Eggs (cooked as preferred), 6
- Pepper and salt to taste

Directions:
- Preheat a big skillet at average heat and put the bacon. Cook bacon till it is crispy or the fat has rendered after which you use a slotted spoon to remove bacon. The bacon is then put on a paper towel and allowed to drain. Decrease the heat to average-low before adding peppers, onions, garlic, sweet potato and mushrooms to the skillet. Coat the mixture by tossing the skillet and allow to cook for 4-7 minutes, stirring just a few times until tender.
- Incorporate the uncooked quinoa to the vegetables and mix, meanwhile allow it to toast slightly. This should take around 3 minutes. Add the water or stock and boil the mixture. Bring to a simmer immediately, secure the lid and cook for about 18 minutes until the quinoa is properly cooked. With the quinoa still cooking, eggs should be prepared as deemed fit. Once done, taste and add seasoning as desired. Quinoa can be served in bowls with cooked bacon and eggs as topping.

APPLE SALAD WITH SLICED BRUSSELS SPROUT

Ingredients
- Shredded Brussels Sprouts, 1 cup
- Julienne sliced apple, ½
- Extra virgin olive oil, 1-2 tablespoons
- Juice from 1 lemon
- Pepper and sea salt to taste
- Pine nuts, ½ cup

Instructions
- Toss all the ingredients in a big bowl. Put some pepper and sea salt to taste.
- Before serving, use pine nuts as topping.
- It is ready to be eaten!

EGG AND ACORN SQUASH BREAKFAST

Ingredients
- Acorn Squash (sliced)
- 4-5 eggs

Instructions
- Put acorn squash in wraps of wet paper towels and heat in a microwave for about 6 minutes. This will help to make the acorn squash tender and make cutting easy. Chop off the top and bottom of acorn squash.
- Cut the squash into sections 1 inch thickness. The oven should be heated to a temperature of 400F. Put wax paper as lining for cooking sheet, then proceed to heat the cooking sheet in the oven for about 7 minutes. Next, the eggs should be cracked with the yolks separated from the egg whites.
- Bring out the cooking sheet from the oven, put slices of acorn on top and spread egg whites equally on individual slices. Ensure the sheet is hot so that egg whites will begin to cook as soon as possible with minimal leakage on the bottom. Place in the oven and bake for about 7 minutes.
- Afterwards, remove sheet from the oven and place yolk individually on each slice and replace in the oven for 2-4 minutes for average and 5-7 for solid done. Season with pepper and a little salt.

FRITTATA SQUASH

Ingredients
- 4 eggs
- Large zucchini (sliced), ½
- Sliced large yellow, ½
- Minced onions, ½ cup
- Parmesan (grated), ½ cup
- Diced garlic, ½ tablespoon
- Salt, ½ teaspoon
- Black pepper, 1 teaspoon
- Olive oil, ½ tablespoon

Instructions
- In cast iron pan, pour little olive oil. Next, layer zucchini and yellow squash. In a big bowl, put garlic, parmesan, pepper, salt, onions and cracked eggs. After beating the eggs, transfer it to the skillet. Firstly heat the oven to about 380F and bake the ingredients for about 24-32 minutes.

LENTIL STEW SWEET POTATO ANDLIMEY CRISPY SALTY TORTILLA BIT POTAGE TOPPERS(HOMEMADE)

Ingredients
- Mini corn tortillas (4-5)
- Cooking spray (nonstick)
- Lime juice, ½
- Sea salt, to taste

Instructions
- Firstly heat oven to Broil. Afterwards, apply nonstick cooking spray on baking sheet and put aside.
- Following step 1, cut mini tortillas into slices with the help of a pizza cutter. Proceed to place them on baking sheet without them touching.
- Use nonstick cooking spray to spray the chips slightly, then top with lemon juice. Sprinkle sea salt as desired.
- Broil one side for around 1-4 minutes, paying close attention. As soon as it starts to brown, bring it out of the oven, turn to the other side, and return back to the oven for extra 2-3 minutes. Ensure you pay close attention once again to prevent them from burning.

SAUSAGE AND ROASTED VEGETABLES

Ingredients
- Spicy sausage, 2 pounds
- Sweet potatoes (medium-sized), 4,peeled and diced
- Bell pepper, 2, diced
- Green bell pepper, 2 diced
- Carrots (peeled and sliced), 4
- Garlic, 5 cloves, diced
- Olive oil, 5 tablespoons
- Thyme, 2 teaspoons
- Basil, 2 teaspoons
- Red pepper flakes, 2 teaspoons
- Pepper and salt, to taste

Instructions
- First heat oven to a temperature of 400F.
- Mix the chopped veggies and sliced sausage in a big bowl. Pour the olive oil, garlic and sprinkle the other seasonings. Coat by tossing the ingredients.
- On a baking sheet lined with foil, spread the mixture. Allow to bake for around 30 minutes at 400F, making sure to turn sausage and veggies halfway through. Once the sweet potatoes are tender, it's ready.
- Serve. Best enjoyed warm.

GIN JAM AND RED PLUM

WHAT YOU NEED
- Red plums, minced, 2 cups
- Water, ½ cup
- Sugar, 1 cup
- Gin, ¼ cup
- Star anise, ½
- Cinnamon stick, ½

WHAT YOU DO
- Pour the cinnamon, sugar, star anise, plums and water into a big pot boil for about 4 minutes.
- Set heat to average-low and cook for additional 7-12 minutes, or till the plums begin to soften.
- Pour the lemon juice and gin and mix properly.
- Take out of the oven, put the pectin, and mix properly.
- Make sure to turn off heat, and put plum jam into sterilized jars.

EASY GUACAMOLE AND PLANTAIN CHIPS PALEO

Ingredients:
- Plantain (green), 1
- Coconut oil, 2-3 tablespoons
- Sea salt
- Garlic, 1 clove
- Avocado, ½
- Lime juice, ½

Instructions:
- Slice plantain, making it as thin as can be achieved.
- In a big cast iron frying pan, melt coconut oil at average heat.
- Pour some of the sliced plantains in one layer (you will have to fry in various batches) and pay close attention as they easily burn.
- Flip them over with a big pancake turner after 2-ish minutes and fry till it is crisp on either side.
- After frying, bring down and allow it to drain on a plate lined with paper towel then add a sprinkling of sea salt. Allow to cool.
- In the meantime, prepare the guacamole. Pound the garlic with salt till it forms a smooth paste (a mortar and pestle can be used for this as I makes it easy).
- Peel the avocado and remove the pit, add it to the garlic. Pour some lime juice then mix properly.
- Taste and add salt as desired.
- Chips will become less crisp over time so serve immediately.

VEGAN WAFFLES-NO GLUTEN

Ingredients:
- Sorghum Flour, 1 cup (or 2½ cups of Superfine Rice Flour)
- Potato Starch, 1 cup
- Potato Flour, 2 teaspoons
- Baking Powder, 3 teaspoons
- Granulated Sugar (whichever brand), 3 tablespoons
- Salt, ½ teaspoon
- Oil (or dairy or non-dairy melted butter), 1 cup
- Milk (dairy or nondairy), 2 cups
- Vinegar or lemon juice, 2½ teaspoons

Instructions:
- Pre-heat waffle maker.
- Combine all the ingredients to make waffle batter
- Spray oil on griddle and pour the batter on the pre-heated griddle. The time is variable. Recipe will give around 12-20 waffles based on the thickness of each waffle.

PALEO CHIVES EGG MUFFINS AND KALE

Ingredients
- 4 eggs
- Coconut milk or almond, ¼ cup
- Finely chopped kale, ½ cup
- Finely chopped chives, ¼ cup
- Pepper and salt to taste
- Prosciutto (optional), 4 slices

Instructions
- Preheat oven to 350
- Firstly whisk eggs before adding the chopped chives and kale. Equally add pepper, salt and the coconut milk/almond. Mix thoroughly.
- Use coconut oil to grease 8 muffin cups or alternatively, use a slice of prosciutto to line each cup.
- Share egg mixture among the 6 muffin cups. Don't completely fill each cup (⅔ recommended) as baking causes the mixture to rise.
- Oven bake for about 25 minutes.
- Allow to cool for a several minutes before lifting out carefully with a fork. You'll observe that the muffins will sink a bit.

PRESSURE COOKER CREAMY RICE PUDDING

Ingredients:
- Arborio rice, 3 cups
- Sugar, 1½ cups
- Salt, 1 teaspoon
- Milk, 8 cups (I used 1%)
- 4 eggs
- Half and half, 2 cups
- Vanilla extract, 3 teaspoons
- Raisins, 2 cups

Directions:
- Mix the milk, salt, rice and sugar in the pressure cooker pot. Saute the mixture and allow to boil, stirring constantly in order to dissolve the sugar. Once the mixture has boiled, cover the pot and secure the lid. Set the pressure cooker to Low Pressure and set timer for 18 minutes.
- With the rice cooking, beat the eggs with vanilla and half and half using a whisker.
- Once the set time has elapsed, turn pressure cooker off, wait for about 12 minutes and then release pressure using quick release. Then carefully remove the lid. Stir the pot of rice.
- Add the egg mixture to the pot and stir. Set the pressure cooker to Saute and cook with the lid remove till the mixture just begins to boil. Turn the pressure cooker off. Stir in the raisins.
- You may serve straight out cooker or cool before chilling in servings dishes. (The longer the pudding cools, the thicker it gets, so a little half and half may be added if you're serving it cold.)

MASHED ACORN CRUSH WITH PRESSURE COOKER

Ingredients
- Stem trimmed acorn squash, cut in two and seeded, 2
- Kosher salt, 2 teaspoons
- Baking soda, ½ teaspoon
- Water, 1 cup

Mix in
- 3 tablespoons of butter
- 3 tablespoons of brown sugar
- 1 teaspoon of grated nutmeg
- Pepper and salt to taste

Directions

Cook squash in pressure cooker
Sprinkle baking soda and kosher salt on cut part of the squash. Place a cooking rack or steaming basket inside the pot, pour a cup of water, and arrange the squash on top. Secure the lid and set the pressure cooker to high pressure. Maintain high pressure by reducing the heat and pressure cook for 23 minutes at high pressure (27 minutes if an electric pressure cooker is used). Release pressure using quick release. Remove squash from the pressure cooker, and allow to cool

Mash the squash
When squash has cooled adequately, remove the flesh of the squash and put it in a medium-sized bowl. Add the brown sugar, nutmeg and sugar. Use a potato masher to mash until the butter is sufficiently melted and the squash becomes smooth. Taste the mashed squash, and pepper and salt as you deem fit.

INSTANT POT BEEF STEW

Ingredients
- Bite-sized chuck roast, 1½ pounds
- Vegetable oil, 1 to 2 tablespoons
- Kosher salt, ½ tablespoon
- Tomato sauce, 8 ounces
- Smoked paprika, ½ teaspoon
- Chicken stock, 8 ounces
- Potatoes (bite-sized), ½ pound
- Carrots (bite-sized), ½ pound
- 1 big onion, cut into bite sized pieces
- Garlic powder, ¼ teaspoon

Instructions
- Sauté bite sized pieces of roast in vegetable oil or brown them in the Instant Pot. Add salt while the meat is browning.
- After the meat has browned, add chicken stock, tomato sauce and smoked paprika. Select soup mode and set timer for 12 minutes.
- Upon completion of the first 'Soup Mode' cycle, add onions, garlic powder, potatoes and carrots to the pot. Set instant pot to 'Soup Mode' for 25 minutes.

INSTANT POT WHOLE CHICKEN

Ingredients
- Whole chicken, 2
- Seasonings as desired
- Water, 2 cups
- Coconut oil, 2 tablespoons

Directions
- Place steam rack inside the Instant Pot and pour two cups of water.
- Heat the oil in a big skillet.
- Add seasoning to the chicken, then put it in the oil and scorch the skin on either side for about two minutes, after which you remove the chicken from heat.
- Put the chicken on the steam rack in the Instant Pot. Secure the lid then set Instant Pot to Chicken (this ought to be done on high pressure) and adjust the time (a little math will be required here, it will take 5 minutes per pound of chicken, then an extra 3 minutes will be added to the total time.
- The chicken should be allowed to steam inside the pot to naturally release for about 20 minutes. The chicken can be kept for longer in the pot, but it should not exceed 25 minutes; that's my recommendation.

DOG MUFFINSWITH MINI CORN

Ingredients

- Melted butter, 1 cup
- Sugar, 1 cup
- 4 eggs
- Buttermilk, 2 cups
- Baking soda, 1 teaspoon
- Gluten-free cornmeal (certified), 2 cups
- All-purpose flour or baking blend (gluten-free), 2 cups
- Salt, 1 teaspoon
- Hot dogs (all-beef), 12-14, cut into 1" bites

Directions

- Oven should be preheated to 375 degrees. Put sugar and butter in a bowl then mix using a whisk. Add eggs then buttermilk, mix both by whisking.
- Combine flour, cornmeal, salt and baking soda in a different bowl, and then combine by stirring. Whisk into wet ingredients in two batches.
- Apply non-stick spray on mini muffin tin then add a tablespoon of batter into each mini muffin cup. Put one hot dog bite into the middle of each cup.
- Bake cornbread until it is golden brown; this should take around 10-15 minutes. Place in a mini muffin tin for about 7 minutes to cool before serving. Store leftovers in the refrigerator then re-heat for 30-40 seconds before serving.

HONEY MUSTARD VEGGIE FRITTATA

Ingredients
- 5 big eggs
- Olive oil or butter, ½ tablespoon
- Nature's Palate Honey Mustard Glaze, 2 tablespoons
- Yellow onion (medium-sized), 1, minced
- 1 big tomato, chopped
- Baby spinach, 2 cups
- Pepper and salt, to taste

Instructions
- Firstly heat oven to 370F.
- Mix honey mustard and eggs in a big bowl. Whisk eggs slightly until they have almost combined. Add pepper and salt.
- Place butter in oven-proof skillet and heat or oil over medium-high heat.*
- Sauté for 4 minutes after adding onions or until it is semitransparent.
- Put the spinach and tomato and continue cooking until spinach is almost limp.
- Top the cooked veggies with egg mixture and cook for about 2 minutes.
- Put the skillet in the oven and bake for about 7-9 minutes or till the top is fairly browned and the eggs are cooked.
- Cool for some time before you proceed to cut into slices.
- Add extra honey mustard glaze to top as you please.

DETOX VEGGIE SOUP

Ingredients
- Olive oil, 2 tablespoons
- Yellow onion (medium), 2, minced
- Big carrot, peeled and chopped, 2
- Chopped celery stalks, 4
- Red bell pepper, 2, chopped
- Garlic cloves, diced, 6
- Green beans, trimmed and chopped, 3 cups
- Minced tomatoes (28-ounce can), 1
- Vegetable stock, 6 cups
- Dried oregano, 3 teaspoons
- Dried basil, 2 teaspoons
- Dried thyme, 1 teaspoon
- Sea salt, 2 teaspoons
- Black pepper, 1 teaspoon
- Stemmed and chopped kale, 6 cups
- Chopped fresh parsley, 4 tablespoons

Instructions
- Preheat a big pot at med-high heat and pour olive oil.
- Add celery, onion and carrot and allow to cook for 4-6 minutes or till the onions are semitransparent.
- Put the bell pepper and garlic and allow it to cook for 2 minutes.
- Put the green beans and allow it to cook for a further two minutes.
- Add vegetable stock, minced tomatoes and spices as topping and mix.
- Boil and then gradually simmer, with the cover removed over med-low heat for about 30 minutes.
- Pour the kale and cook for additional 7 minutes; the kale will become limp.
- Use fresh parsley to top and serve warm.
- It will last for up to a week in a refrigerator, and can keep for a few months.

EGG BREAKFAST & ACORN SQUASH

Ingredients
- Diced Acorn Squash
- 8 to10 eggs

Direction
- The acorn squash should be wrapped in paper towels that are went and put in a microwave for about 6 minutes to make is easy soft. The top and bottom should be cut off. The squash should be cut into pieces with thickness of about 1 ½ inches. The oven should be heated earlier to 400°F degrees. The cooking sheet should be arranged with heat sheet and wax paper for around 7 minutes. The eggs should be cracked with the yolk separated. The heated cooking sheet should be taken out from the heat put the slices of acorn on it and share the white parts of the egg be placed well on every slice. Ensure the sheet is hot to make the egg start burning immediately. Bake it for about 7 minutes inside the oven. Each separate yolk should be put into every slice then put back for it to heat again for about 6 to 8 minutes for it to be properly done. To make it flavor add a pinch of pepper and salt.

CPSIA information can be obtained
at www.ICGtesting.com
Printed in the USA
FFOW04n0438271216
30770FF